D1144742

death
at my doorstep

OTHER LOTUS TITLES:

FORTHCOMING TITLES:

KHUSHWANT SINGH

OBITUARIES

death

at my doorstep

LOTUS COLLECTION
ROLI BOOKS

COVENTRY CITY LIBRARIES	
201553174	
Bertrams	05.02.08
Lotus Collection 920.02	£11.99
CEN	

© Mala Dayal 2005
All rights reserved. No part of this publication may be
reproduced or transmitted, in any form or by any means,
without the prior permission of the publisher.

This edition first published in 2005

Sixth impression 2006
The Lotus Collection
An imprint of
Roli Books Pvt. Ltd.
M-75, G.K. II Market
New Delhi 110 048
Phones: ++91 (011) 2921 2271, 2921 2782
2921 0886; Fax: ++91 (011) 2921 7185
E-mail: roli@vsnl.com; Website: rolibooks.com
Also at
Bangalore, Varanasi, Jaipur and the Netherlands

Cover Design: Arati Subramanyam
Layout Design: Kumar Raman
Cover Photograph: Sharad Saxena

ISBN: 81-7436-356-4
Rs 295/-

Typeset in Fairfield LH Light by Roli Books Pvt. Ltd. and
printed at Tan Prints (India) Pvt. Ltd., Jhajjar, Haryana

FOR JAYA THADANI
whose letters sustained
my spirits in my later years

CONTENTS

ACKNOWLEDGEMENTS

The idea of putting together a book on obituaries was suggested by Pramod Kapoor of Roli Books. It appealed to me immensely, and after giving it some thought, I decided to name the book *Death at My Doorstep*: it gave me the opportunity to spell out my views on death and dying which I felt was appropriate for a man in his 90s—besides other people's obituaries, I could also write my own.

Most of the spadework for *Death at My Doorstep* was done by Dipa Chaudhuri of Roli Books. She painstakingly went through a considerable body of my writings including past issues of *The Illustrated Weekly of India, New Delhi, The Hindustan Times* and *The Tribune,* as well as my collection of short stories *The Mark of Vishnu* (Saturn Press and Ravi Dayal), where some of these pieces had first appeared, and selected what she liked. But for her this book would not have seen the light of day.

Sunset and evening star
And one clear call for me!
May there be no moaning of the bar
When I put out to sea...

...Twilight and evening bell,
After that the dark!
And may there be no sadness of farewell
When I embark.

—ALFRED LORD TENNYSON

PREFACE.

We do not talk of death lightly—it is regarded as tasteless, ill-mannered and depressing. This is the wrong way to look upon an essential fact of life which makes no exceptions: It comes to kings as well as beggars, to the rich and the poor, to saints as well as sinners, the aged and the young. You simply cannot turn a blind eye to it and fool yourself into believing that death comes to other people but will spare you. It will not. It is best to prepare yourself for it and when it comes, welcome it with a smile on your lips.

I am now over 90 years old and am aware that the hour of my tryst with destiny is drawing near. I have given a lot of thought to it. Being a rationalist, I do not accept irrational, unproven theories of life-death-rebirth in different forms as an unending process till our beings mingle with God and we attain nirvana. I do not accept the belief that while the body perishes, the soul survives. I do not know what the soul looks like; neither I, nor anyone has seen it. Nor do I accept the Hebrew, Christian and Islamic belief in the Day of Judgement—heaven and hell. I go along with the poet Mirza Asadullah Khan Ghalib when he said:

Hum ko maaloom hai Jannat kee haqeeqat leykin,
Dil kay khush rakhney ko Ghalib, yeh khayaal achha hai.

(We know what the reality of paradise is;
   but it is not too bad an idea to beguile the mind.)

As far as I am concerned, I accept the finality of death; we do not
know what happens to us after we die.

I have put my views as well as those of others on the subject as
honestly as I could. I have also added obituaries of people I met—
some were well known, others humble non-entities. Many of these
were published in the two syndicated columns I have been writing
every week for many years: 'This Above All' in *The Tribune* and 'With
Malice Towards One and All' in *The Hindustan Times*.

I have never subscribed to the belief that nothing bad should be
said about the dead. If people were evil in their lifetimes, death does
not convert them into saints. Such falsehoods may be condoned
when inscribed on tombstones but not in obituaries which should be
without bias, and truthful. I have written lots of obituaries about
people I admired and loved; I have also written about people I
detested and loathed. I did my best to be as even-handed as I could
about all of them. I was accused of maligning people who could not
hit back or take me to court for libel. It is true that there are no
provisions in our law for friends or relatives of a dead person to take
an author to court on a charge of libel unless that libel hurts their
reputations. But I have written scathing profiles of eminent men
including governors of states. Two of them took me to court and the
Press Council. In both cases, the matter was settled by compromise
requiring me to say that I did not intend to hurt their feelings—
which in fact I did.

I have written obituaries of myself. The first entitled *Posthumous*
was written when I was still in my twenties and appeared in a
collection of my short stories, *The Mark of Vishnu* published by
Saturn Press in London. I take the liberty of reproducing it here to
prove that death need not necessarily be a matter to cry over and can
be a subject of jest as well.

* * *

Posthumous

I am in bed with fever. It is not serious. In fact, it is not serious at all,
as I have been left alone to look after myself. I wonder what would
happen if the temperature suddenly shot up. Perhaps I would die.
That would be really hard on my friends. I have so many and am so
popular. I wonder what the paper would have to say about it. They
couldn't just ignore me. Perhaps *The Tribune* would mention it on its
front page with a small photograph. The headline would read 'Sardar
Khushwant Singh Dead'—and then in somewhat smaller print:

> We regret to announce the sudden death of Sardar Khushwant Singh at
> 6 p.m. last evening. He leaves behind a young widow, two infant
> children and a large number of friends and admirers to mourn his loss.
> It will be recalled that the Sardar came to settle in Lahore some five
> years ago from his hometown, Delhi. Within these years he rose to a
> position of eminence in the Bar and in politics. His loss will be mourned
> generally throughout the province.
>
> Amongst those who called at the late Sardar's residence were the
> P.A. to the Chief Justice, several Ministers, and Judges of the High
> Court.
>
> In the statement to the press, the Hon'ble Chief Justice said: 'I feel
> that the Punjab is poorer by the passing away of this man. The cruel
> hand of death has cut short the promise of a brilliant career.'

At the bottom of the page would be an announcement:

> The funeral will take place at 10 a.m. today.

I feel very sorry for myself and for all my friends. With difficulty I
check the tears which want to express sorrow at my own death. But
I also feel elated and want people to mourn me. So I decide to die—
just for the fun of it as it were. In the evening, giving enough time for
the press to hear of my death, I give up the ghost. Having emerged

from my corpse, I come down and sit on the cool marble steps at the entrance to wallow in posthumous glory.

In the morning I get the paper before my wife. There is no chance of a squabble over the newspaper as I am downstairs already, and in any case my wife is busy pottering around my corpse. *The Tribune* lets me down. At the bottom of page 3, column 1, I find myself inserted in the little brackets of obituary notices of retired civil servants—and that is all. I feel annoyed. It must be that blighter Shafi, Special Representative. He never liked me. But I couldn't imagine he would be so mean as to deny me a little importance when I was dead. However, he wouldn't keep the wave of sorrow which would run over the province from trickling into his paper. My friends would see to that.

Near the High Court the paper is delivered fairly early. In the house of my lawyer friend Qadir it is deposited well before dawn. It isn't that the Qadirs are early risers. As a matter of fact, hardly anyone stirs in the house before 9 a.m. But Qadir is a great one for principle and he insists that the paper must be available early in the morning even if it is not looked at.

As usual, the Qadirs were in bed at 9 a.m. He had worked very late at night. She believed in sleep anyhow. The paper was brought in on a tray along with a tumbler of hot water with a dash of lime juice. Qadir sipped the hot water between intervals of cigarette smoking. He had to do this to make his bowels work. He only glanced at the headlines in bed. The real reading was done when the cigarette and lime had their effect. The knowledge of how fate had treated me had to await the lavatory.

In due course, Qadir ambled into the bathroom with the paper in one hand and a cigarette perched on his lower lips. Comfortably seated, he began to scan it thoroughly and his eyes fell on news of lesser import. When he got to page 3, column 1, he stopped smoking for a moment, a very brief moment. Should he get up and shout to his wife? No, he decided, that would be an unnecessary demonstration. Qadir was a rationalist. He had become more of one since he married a woman who was a bundle of emotions and explosions. The poor fellow was dead and nothing could be done about it. He knew his wife would burst out crying when he told her. That was all the more reason that he should be matter-of-fact about it—just as if he was going to tell her of a case he had lost.

Qadir knew his wife well. He told her with an air of casualness, and she burst out crying. Her ten-year-old daughter came running into the room. She eyed his mother for a little while and then joined her in the wailing. Qadir decided to be severe.

'What are you making all this noise for?' he said sternly. 'Do you think it will bring him back to life?'

His wife knew that it was no use arguing with him. He always won the arguments.

'I think we should go to their house at once. His wife must be feeling wretched,' she said.

Qadir shrugged his shoulders.

'I am afraid I cannot manage it. Much as I would like to condole with his wife—or rather widow—my duty to my clients comes first. I have to be at the tribunal in half an hour.'

Qadir was at the tribunal all day and his family stayed at home.

Not far from the city's big park lives another friend, Khosla. He and his family, consisting of a wife, three sons and a daughter, reside in this upper-class residential area. He is a judge and very high up in the bureaucracy.

Khosla is an early riser. He has to rise early because that is the only time he has to himself. During the day he has to work in the court. In the evenings he plays tennis—and then he has to spend some time with the children and fussing with his wife. He has a large number of visitors, as he is very popular and enjoys popularity. But Khosla is ambitious. As a lad he had fancied himself as a clever boy. In his early youth hair had begun to fall off and had uncovered a large bald pate. Kholsa had looked upon it as nature's confirmation of his opinion about himself. Perhaps he was a genius. The more he gazed upon his large head in the mirror, the more he became convinced that fate had marked for him an extraordinary career. So he worked harder. He won scholarships and rounded off his academic career by topping the list in the Civil Service examination. He had justified the confidence he had in himself by winning laurels in the stiffest competitive examination in the country. For some years he lived the life of a contented bureaucrat. In fact, he assured himself that he was what people called 'a success in life'.

After some years this contentment had vanished. Every time he brushed the little tuft at the back of his head and ran his hands across his vast forehead, he became conscious of unrealized expectations. There were hundreds of senior civil servants like him. All were considered successes in life. The Civil Service was obviously not enough. He would work—he would write—he knew he could write. There it was written in the size of his head. So Khosla took to writing. In order to write well he took to reading. He amassed a large library and regularly spent some hours in it before going to work.

This morning Khosla happened to be in a mood to write. He made himself a cup of tea and settled in a comfortable armchair by the electric radiator. He stuck the pencil in his mouth and meditated. He couldn't think of what to write. He decided to write his diary. He had spent the previous day listening to an important case. It was likely to go on for some days. The courtroom had been packed and everyone had been looking at him—that seemed a good enough subject. So he started to write.

Khosla was disturbed by the knock of the bearer bringing in the paper. He opened the newssheet to read the truths of mundane existence.

Khosla was more interested in social affairs, births, marriages and deaths, than events of national or international import. He turned to page 3, column 1. His eye caught the announcement and he straightened up.

He just tapped his notebook with his pencil, and after a wake-up cough, informed his wife of the news. She just yawned and opened her large dreamy eyes wide.

'I suppose you will close the High Court today?' she said

'I am afraid the High Court doesn't close at just any excuse. I'll have to go. If I have any time I'll drop in on the way—or we can call on Sunday.'

The Khoslas did not come. Nor did many others for whose sorrow at my demise I had already felt sorrowful.

At 10 o'clock a little crowd had collected in front of the open space beneath my flat. It consisted mainly of people I did not expect to see. There were some lawyers in their court dress, and a number of sightseers who wanted to find out what was happening. Two friends of mine also turned up, but they stood apart from the crowd. One was a tall, slim man who looked like an artist. With one hand he kept his cigarette in place, the other he constantly employed in pushing his long hair off his forehead. He was a writer. He did not believe in attending funerals. But one had to hang around for a little while as a sort of social obligation. It was distasteful to him. There was something infectious about a corpse—so he smoked incessantly and made a cigarette smoke-screen between himself and the rest of the world.

The other friend was a Communist, a short, slight man with wavy hair and a hawkish expression. His frame and expression belied the volcano which they camouflaged. His approach to everything was coldly Marxist and sentiment found no place in it. Deaths were unimportant events. It was the cause that mattered. He consulted the writer in a polite whisper.

'How far are you going?'

'I plan dropping off at the coffee house,' answered the other. 'Are you going the whole way?'

'No ruddy fear,' said the Communist emphatically. 'Actually I had to be at a meeting at 10 and I was planning to be free of this by 9.30—but you know our people haven't the foggiest idea about time. I'll get along to the Party office now and then meet you at the coffee house at 11.30. Incidentally if you get the opportunity, just ask the hearse driver if he is a member of the Tongawalla Union. Cheers.'

A little later, a hearse, drawn by a bony brown horse arrived and pulled up in front of my doorstep. The horse and his master were completely oblivious of the solemnity of the occasion. The driver sat placidly chewing his betel nut and eyeing the assembly. He was wondering whether this was the type likely to produce a tip. The beast straightway started to piddle and the crowd scattered to avoid the spray which rebounded off the brick floor.

The crowd did not have to wait very long. My corpse was brought down all tied up in white linen and placed inside the hearse. A few flowers were ceremoniously placed on me. The procession was ready to start.

Before we moved, another friend turned up on his bicycle. He was somewhat dark and flabby. He carried several books on the carrier and had the appearance of a scholarly serious-minded professor. As soon as he saw the loaded hearse, he dismounted. He had great respect for the dead and was particular to express it. He put his bicycle in the hall, chained it, and joined the crowd. When my wife came down to bid her last farewell, he was visibly moved. From his pocket he produced a little book and thoughtfully turned over its pages. Then he slipped through the people towards my wife. With tears in his eyes he handed the book to her.

'I've brought you a copy of the *Gita*. It will give you great comfort.'

Overcome with emotion, he hurriedly slipped back to wipe the tears which had crept into his eyes.

'This,' he said to himself with a sigh, 'is the end of human existence. This is the truth.'

He was fond of thinking in platitudes—but to him all platitudes were profound and had the freshness and vigour of original thought.

'Like bubbles,' he said to himself, 'human life is as momentary as a bubble.'

But one didn't just die and disappear. Matter could not immaterialize—it could only change its form. The *Gita* put it so beautifully...

'Like a man casts off old garments to put on new ones…so does the soul, etc., etc.'

The professor was lost in contemplation. He wondered what new garments his dead friend had donned.

His thoughts were disturbed by a movement between his legs. A little pup came round the professor's legs licking his trousers and looking up at him. The professor was a kind man. He involuntarily bent down and patted the little dog, allowing him to lick his hands.

The professor's mind wandered—he felt uneasy. He looked at the corpse and then at the fluffy little dog at his feet, who after all was part of God's creation.

'Like a man casts off old garments to put on new ones…so does the soul…'

No, no, he said to himself. He shouldn't allow such uncharitable thoughts to cross his mind. But he couldn't check his mind. It wasn't impossible. The *Gita* said so, too. And he bent down again and patted the little dog with more tenderness and fellow feeling.

The procession was on the move. I was in front, uncomfortably laid within the glass hearse, with half a dozen people walking behind. It went down towards the river.

By the time it had passed the main street, I found myself in solitude. Some of the lawyers had left at the High Court. My author friend had branched off to the coffee house, still smoking. At the local college, the professor gave me a last longing, lingering look and sped up the slope to his classroom. The remaining six or seven disappeared into the District Courts.

I began to feel a little small. Lesser men than myself had larger crowds. Even a dead pauper carried on a municipal wheelbarrow got two sweepers to cart him off. I had only one human being, the driver, and even he seemed to be oblivious of the enormity of the soul whose decayed mansion he was transporting on its last voyage. As for the horse, he was positively rude.

The route to the cremation ground is marked with an infinite variety of offensive smells. The climax is reached when one has to branch off the main road towards the crematorium along a narrow path which runs beside the city's one and only sewer. It is a stream of dull, black fluid with bubbles bursting on its surface all the time.

Fortunately for me, I was given some time to ruminate over my miscalculated posthumous importance. The driver pulled up under a large peepul tree near where the road turns off to the cremation ground. Under this peepul tree is a tonga stand and a water trough for horses to drink out of. The horse made for the water and the driver clambered off his perch to ask the tonga-drivers for a light for his cigarette.

The tonga-drivers gathered round the hearse and peered in from all sides. 'Must be someone rich,' said one. 'But there is no one with him,' queried another. 'I suppose this is another English custom—no one to go with funerals.'

By now I was thoroughly fed up. There were three ways open to me. One was to take the route to the cremation ground and, like the others that went there, give myself up to scorching flames, perhaps to be born again into a better world, but probably to be extinguished into nothingness. There was another road which forked off to the right towards the city. There lived harlots and other people of ill-repute. They drank and gambled and fornicated. Theirs was a world of sensation and they crammed their lives with all the varieties which the senses were capable of registering. The third one was to take the way back. It was difficult to make up one's mind. In situations like these the toss of a coin frequently helps. So I decided to toss the coin; heads and I hazard the world beyond; tails and I go to join the throng of sensation seekers in the city; if it is neither heads nor tails and the coin stands on its edge, I retrace my steps to a humdrum existence bereft of the spirit of adventure and denuded of the lust of living.

1943

* * *

In 1948 I was the Press Officer in charge of Public Relations with the Indian High Commission in London. Krishna Menon was the High Commissioner. One day the evening paper carried the news of the death of Her Highness, the Rani of Mandi with her photographs on their front cover. It was evident she was a young and beautiful woman when she died.

The next morning when I was in my office, I had a visitor. He was a tall Englishman dressed in a black top hat, black coat and tie, and striped trousers. He introduced himself: 'I am Mr. Kenyon of Kenyon & Kenyon Undertakers. No doubt you have heard of us.'

Indeed I had. I had seen their offices in different parts of London with polished oak coffins and vases of white lilies in their show windows. They were the biggest firm of undertakers in England. I assured Mr. Kenyon that I was well aware of their importance.

'Thank you, Sir,' he replied and put a parcel he was carrying on my table. 'Sir,' he continued, 'you must have read of the death of Her Highness, the Rani of Mandi?'

I told him I had seen it in the previous day's evening paper.

'Sad, wasn't it?' he said pulling a long face.

'Very sad,' I replied also pulling a long face.

Mr Kenyon proceeded to open the parcel he had brought and continued, 'Sir, although we have considerable experience in preparing those who have passed on for their burial or cremation, this assignment is new to us.' He undid the strings of the parcel and took out a gorgeous orange-coloured silk sari with a gold border. 'Her Highness left a will to the effect that on her cremation, her body was to be draped in her favourite sari that she had worn for her wedding. Despite our vast experience, we have no idea how Indian ladies drape their saris. I took the liberty of coming to ask for your help in the matter.'

Without a pause I replied, 'I am sorry Mr Kenyon, though I have some experience of taking saris off, I have none of putting them on.'

Mr. Kenyon was deeply offended. He put the sari back in the parcel, drew himself up to his full height of six foot and some inches, put on his black top hat and marched out of my room saying, 'Good day to you, Sir.'

He went straight up to the High Commissioner's office on the third floor and lodged a complaint against my boorish behaviour. After he had got instructions on how to drape a sari from a bevy of Indian girls working in the High Commission's typing pool and left, I was summoned by the High Commissioner.

'Sardar, can't you restrain yourself from trying to be damn witty?' Then he beamed a broad smile at me.

Part 1

ON DEATH AND DYING

THE DALAI LAMA ON DEATH

'I do not believe in reincarnation nor in the Day of Judgement followed by heaven or hell. There is no scientific proof for one or the other. For me death is the final full stop.' I said, 'What is your reaction to this statement?'

The Dalai Lama had a hearty laugh before he replied, 'As for myself I say the choice is yours to accept or reject what you like and believe what you like. It is entirely your business.'

I protested. 'Isn't it more honest to admit that you don't know what happens after death?'

The Dalai Lama relented. 'All you need to be is a good and honest person. There is no need to argue about that.'

'But I am frightened of death. Life is full of pleasant things. I don't want to lose it.'

'It is also full of miseries,' he added.

'Yes,' I conceded. 'But they don't afflict me just yet. When they do I may not want to live. Right now, I don't want to go. How do I conquer this fear of dying?'

'There are many things we don't know about death. For example, memory. With the body go mental faculties, but there remains another factor which is beyond brain cells. Last year,

scientists carried out an experiment on a practitioner of
Buddhism. Through concentration or meditation he had
stopped breathing for a full 40 minutes.

'I am not sure whether his heart stopped beating. But he
could not be declared dead because he revived. It proved that
there is something beyond the brain—it may be mind or
energy. The brain ceases to function, not the mind. You can
train that energy. It is this that gives some people clear
perception of their past lives.' He gave me instances of two
girls, one from Ambala, the other from Kanpur, who had clear
perceptions of their past lives. 'Now they have four sets of
parents each: two in this life, two of their past lives. Such
things happen. There is my own story. Therefore we believe in
reincarnation. Because it happens, we regard it as scientific
proof and accept it. Today's body is a continuation of
yesterday's body. A newborn child is a continuation of the
unborn child right to the moment of conception—and to the
father's sperm entering the mother's egg. Conception does not
always follows. There is a third factor which is the mind or
consciousness which gives it continuity.'

He illustrated his point by pointing to the teapot with hot
water. Its hotness was caused by being exposed to fire; it could
freeze if exposed to cold. But it could not be either hot or cold
without the continuity of water being there. It is the same with
the body and mind. Without a previous mind the present mind
could not exist.

I posed my last, unscheduled question: 'Why do people
pray? Even murderers pray for success before they go on their
murderous missions. Most people pray for money or good
health.'

'Buddhists regard prayer as an appeal to a higher being for
guidance. Its effect is limited. Ultimately a man is responsible
for his own actions. If one does wrong, even the Buddha
cannot help him. Everyone is his own master.'

I returned to the subject of death and life thereafter. 'Your Holiness, I know Buddhists regard the existence of God as an open question. I go along with that. But I cannot accept your belief in reincarnation. There is no scientific evidence to support it.'

The Dalai Lama again narrated stories of children who remembered things about their previous existence: names of parents and places where they were born...

I interrupted him. 'Your Holiness, these are infantile fantasies of children brought up in Hindu, Jain, Buddhist or Sikh families where they hear elders talking of *pichchla janam* (previous life), *agla janam* (next life). Can you give me an example of a Muslim child recalling his earlier existence?'

The Dalai Lama roared with laughter and replied, 'You have a point there! But if I did not believe in reincarnation, I would be out of business!'

FEAR OF DYING: ACHARYA RAJNEESH

The only time I met Acharya Rajneesh, I asked him about death. There was nothing very profound about our dialogue as it did not go beyond restatement of platitudes—knowing death is inevitable, why do we fear it? Is there any way of overcoming the phobia? Do we know anything about what happens to us after we die? And so on. The Acharya has now put all his thoughts on the subject together in a small 100-page booklet entitled *Death: The Greatest Fiction*. For once I am disappointed with his treatment of a serious and disturbing topic. Death is not a fiction; it is a profound reality, more real than anything in life.

The Acharya has an inimitable style of simplifying the most abstruse themes and illustrating them with pithy anecdotes. The offhand way in which he mocks the pretensions of prophets and philosophers is refreshing. But this time, he is unconvincing.

He starts his discourse by narrating his first exposure to death. He was only seven years old. He was taking his sick grandfather to hospital in a bullock cart with only his grandmother and the cart driver as his companions. On the way, the grandfather, barely 50, gave up the ghost. His last words were: 'My Lord, this life you have given me, I surrender it back to you with my thanks.' None in the cart shed a tear. When told that her old man had stopped breathing, the grandmother reassured Rajneesh, 'That's perfectly okay, as he had lived enough; there is no need to ask for more... Remember, because these are the moments not to be forgotten, never ask for more. What is, is enough.' Then she burst into a song.

Acharya assures us that death is not the end of a man's journey but a door to God. The death of a loved one certainly creates a vacuum but since life itself is meaningless, there is nothing to mourn about. One should not fear death but regard it as a long, relaxed sleep from which you wake up to a brighter dawn. He writes: 'People who are afraid of death cannot relax in sleep, because sleep is also a very small death that comes every day. People who are afraid of death are also afraid of love, because love is a death. People who are afraid of death become afraid of all orgasmic experiences, because in each orgasm, the ego dies.'

I am out of my depth. I am not afraid of love; I also regard an orgasm as the ultimate in physical exaltation. Yet I fear death.

The Acharya proceeds to make further assertions which leave me flabbergasted. He asserts that a dying man sees in a flash his entire life. But if he has unfulfilled desires, they will decide his future life. 'So what you do at the moment of your death determines how your birth is going to be,' he says.

I go along with Rajneesh when he says that life should be lived as intensely as possible (though this would seem to contradict his earlier statement that life is meaningless), but I fail to comprehend what he means when he says, 'In my religion, death is celebrated because there is no death. It is only an entry into another life.' He faults the Hebraic family of religions (Judaism, Christianity and Islam) for believing in only one life. That, according to him, is why Westerners who subscribe to these religions are always in a hurry to get things done and have never grasped the concept of meditation.

Whereas Indians, because they believe in rebirth, don't feel the pressure of time, are non-achievers but meditative.

'Religion only has validity because of death,' says Acharya Rajneesh. 'If there is no death, nobody would have bothered about religion at all.' He is right on the track there. But why then is religion, in all its spurious manifestations, more in evidence in India where the vast majority believe in reincarnation than elsewhere? What evidence has he for saying that death is a 'beautiful sleep, a dreamless sleep, a sleep that is needed for you to enter into another body, silently and peacefully'? He goes on to reassert that 'those who die unconsciously will be born on some other planet, in some other womb.'

It is not fair on the part of the Acharya to ask us to take his word and accept the theory of transmigration of souls. 'It is my experience... When I say that the soul transmigrates, to me it is an experience. I remember my past lives. I have transmigrated; there is no question of doubt for me, but I am not saying for you to believe it.' He talks of *déjà vu* (already seen)—an experience some people have when they visit a new place. They feel they have been there before because they have in fact done so in their previous lives. No sceptic or rationalist will buy this argument.

I go along with the Acharya in his general approach to life. He says: 'These are the "three Ls" of my *philosophia*: life, love, laughter. Life is only a seed, love is a flower, laughter is a fragrance. Just to be born is not enough, one has to learn the art of living; that is the A of meditation. Then one has to learn the art of loving; that is the B of meditation. And then one has to learn the art of laughing; that is the C of meditation. And meditation has only three letters: A, B, C.'

It is difficult to accept the Acharya's views on death. Having allowed himself to become a Bhagwan, he has forfeited the right to say, 'I do not know.' Nobody, not even Bhagwan Rajneesh, knows what happens to us when we die. And as long as we do not know, we will continue to dread it.

HAVE YOU EVER THOUGHT OF DEATH?

Retired Commissioner of Income Tax, S. Prasher, the moving spirit behind the Save Kasauli Society has this disturbing habit of tossing questions at me to which I have no answers. This was the second time he asked me: 'Have you ever thought about death?'

'Indeed I have,' I replied. 'I think about it all the time. I've read as much about it as I could. I found no answers.' I quoted my favourite lines on the subject:

There was a door to which I found no key,
There was a veil beyond which I could not see;
Talk awhile of Thee and me there was
Then no more of Thee or me.

'Omar Khayyam!' he said triumphantly. 'But surely there is more to it than just admitting you do not know. The body goes, perhaps with it the mind as well. Your memory remains in some people's minds while they are alive. After them even that is gone. You may leave charitable trusts in your name, you may write books that may be read after you are gone. That is not what I mean. What about consciousness?'

'Consciousness of what?' I asked. 'Where does it survive? It has to be something more tangible than the notion of consciousness.'

He proceeded to explain at great length. Most of it was beyond my comprehension. I tried to bring him down to earth. 'Most thinkers play with words, some talk of death as an integral part of life. I agree. Some compare life as a journey on a train; some get off at one station, others continue a little further. Bhola Nathji in his *The Secret of Death* writes: "One can deny the existence of God, but one cannot deny the existence of death... Life is that which must go, and death, that which must come." I entirely agree, but does that tell us where we go when we die? Does anything of us remain when we are gone?'

Most people who have written on the subject have dwelt more on the inherent fear of dying rather than death. They give false assurances that death is nothing to be scared of. John Donne (1573-1631) describes it as 'merely a form of rest and sleep': 'Death, be not proud, though some have called thee Mighty and dreadful, for thou art not so; For those whom thou thinkest thou dost overthrow, Die not, poor Death; not yet canst thou kill me.' For Donne, death was, 'One short sleep past, we wake eternally. And death shall be no more: Death thou shalt die.' Brave words like those of a man shouting loudly in the dark when he is frightened of ghosts. John Keats (1795-1821) who died at the young age of twenty-six had no such illusions of something surviving after he 'ceased to be'. He knew that he had a lot more to give but felt he was the 'fair creature of an hour' after which love and fame would 'sink to nothingness'. The key word, I tell Prasher, is nothingness. Death erases our bodies, minds and everything our bodies or minds may have achieved in our lives. Prasher is not satisfied with my answers. But he has no answers to offer besides conjecturing that consciousness remains. Where? In the air or empty spaces? He exhorts me to think more deeply on the subject. I promise to do so fully aware of the fact it will get me nowhere.

BE PREPARED

Very few people have dates with death apart from those who take their own lives or are convicted by courts to hang. The old and the ailing may sense that the day is drawing near but never know exactly what day or time it will be. Most of us go through near-death experiences as and when we travel by buses, trains, planes which later crash. I have written about some of mine like driving away a few seconds before a huge branch of a tree under which I had parked my car crashed as a sudden dust storm blew over. I was also on the hit list of Khalistani terrorists; unknown to me, one even took a look inside my flat and followed me up to Kasauli where he sensed he was being shadowed by the police. On his return to Delhi he was nabbed and later hanged in Pune jail for a murder he had committed earlier.

We must always bear in mind that death is inevitable. *Memento mori*—remember you must die. Without brooding over it be prepared for it. The poet Asadullah Khan Ghalib put it beautifully:

Rau mein hai rakhsh-e-umar kahaan deykheeye thammey?
Nai haath baag par hai nah pa hai rakaab mein.

(Age travels at a galloping pace
Who knows where it will stop?
We do not have the reins in our hands
We do not have our feet in the stirrups.)

I had one near-death experience year before last in Kasauli. I was 88 but in reasonably good shape for my age. I took a variety of pills morning and evening to fight off old-age ailments; fluctuating blood pressure, enlarged prostate gland, malfunctioning of the liver—and that sort of thing. It was late monsoon time and there was a lot of humidity in the air. I was not aware that the caches of pills had caught fungus and become ineffective.

One afternoon after I got up after my siesta, gathered my shawl and scribbling pad, and proceeded towards the verandah which opened into the garden where I usually stayed till sunset, I felt the roof crash down on my head, and the books in the bookshelves came tumbling down on me. I fell flat on my face grazing my forehead and my nose. For a while I lay sprawled on the floor. There was no one around at that hour I could call for help. I could not get up. I crawled on the floor like a crab trying to find a ledge or piece of furniture I could grab and haul myself up. I thought my end had come. Then I thought of the many assignments I had to fulfil. I would be letting down my publishers and editors of papers for whom I had been writing for over 60 years without ever missing the deadline. I did not pray for a little more time. I recalled Allama Iqbal's stirring lines:

Baagh-e-bahisht say mujhay hukm-e-safar diya thha kyon?
Kaar-e-Jahaan daraaz hai, ab meyra intazaar kar.

(Why did you order me out of the garden of paradise?
I have a lot of work that remains unfulfilled; now you better wait for me.)

I told the *Badey Mian* (the Big Boss) sitting in the clouds that I had no *fursat* (leisure) to come to Him. And it was now for Him to await my coming.

I managed to grab a leg of my bed and pick myself up. I sent for Dr Kutty to ask him what had gone wrong. He took my blood pressure—it was dangerously low. He examined the pills I was taking and pronounced them useless. He gave me a mixture of salt and sugar. I live to tell my tale.

Everyone should prepare himself or herself for the inevitable end. For whatever it is worth, I make a few practical suggestions which may help a person to go at peace with himself and the world. It you are a man of property do not overlook making a will while you are of sound mind and body. If you are in service, it is best to do so on retirement. Show your will to your beneficiaries and gain their approval while you are alive so that they do not squabble between themselves after you are gone. If you wish to leave money for your servants, staff or friends or for charity, it is best to do so in your lifetime and not leave it to your beneficiaries to honour your commitments. For too often they neglect to do so.

Start getting rid of your possessions. Restrict your bank account to what you need for your monthly expenses with something in reserve for contingencies like doctor's fees, medicines, hospital bills if you are hospitalized. And your funeral expenses. Clear all your debts: you should not be owing anything to anyone when you go. Your financial slate should be as clean as possible: little on the credit side, nothing on the debit side.

The same applies to your personal possessions like watches, pens, radio, TV sets, extra suits, ties, turbans, shirts, etc. Keep only what is essential for your preoccupations, keep reminding yourself that you cannot take anything with you.

Cut down your social life to the very minimum. Partying is for the young who have plenty of time to waste drinking and indulging in small talk. You no longer have much time to waste. Do your best to take *Sanyas* in your own home with creative comforts, eat only easily digestible wholesome food, drink only good Scotch and wine. Also distance yourself from those you love and cherish without hurting their feelings. Remember that on your last journey to the unknown beyond, there will be no one with you.

Cultivate solitude: in solitude is bliss. If you have hobbies like gardening, growing bonsai, reading books, watching birds and trees and the change of seasons, you will discover that you can be alone without being lonely.

Above all, when the time comes to go, go like a man without any regret or grievances against anyone. Allama Iqbal put it beautifully in a couplet in Persian:

Nishaan-e-mard-e-Momin ba too goyam?
Choon marg aayad, tabassum bar lab-e-ost.

(You ask me about the signs of a man of faith?
When death comes to him, he has a smile on his lips.)

ON THE HIT LIST

One day last week I received in my mail a printed leaflet stating that all its recipients and every member of their families would be eliminated within ten days as we had been declared enemies of Khalistan. In the last four years, I have received many such threats in writing and over the telephone. This was the first one in print and the first one setting a time limit to my existence: the earlier ones were largely abusive and warned me to pack up my belongings for the eternal journey: *boree bistra gol kar lai or taino sodh diyangay* (pack your bags and we will put you on the right path).

I have learnt to live with this kind of thing without losing my sleep. At my age I would prefer a quick exit to months of wasting away in some hospital ward suffering the indignity of having bedpans stuck under my bottom—and gain the halo of martyrdom to boot.

I am not indulging in bravado. Though a Sikh, I am somewhat of a coward. I know, as do most of my would-be killers, that the bullet is the last argument of a person who knows he has lost the debate. Let me assure them that if they labour under any illusion that threats will deter me from writing what I have been against Khalistan as hara-kiri of the Khalsa Panth, they are sadly mistaken. I will prove, if I must, that the pen is still mightier than the sword, a Kalashnikov or a self-loading rifle.

However, some aspects of the printed leaflet depressed me. They couldn't have gone to the extent of printing just one leaflet for me: hundreds, perhaps thousands of others must have received them. My name must be way down their hit list. They will only come for me when they fail to get somebody more important. I find that wounding to my self-esteem. If I have to be on a hit list, I would like my name to be on the top. Perhaps my would-be liquidators would do me this last honour.

NEARING DEATH: OLD AGE

A sizeable part of my mail consists of letters from gentlemen who describe themselves as senior citizens and pensioners. Their general tenor is that nothing is being done in the country for old people who are unable to fend for themselves. Most of them are from men in their late 60s and 70s; a few from octogenarians. I write back expressing my lack of sympathy. I am as old as most of them, if not older. In my 70s I am working harder than I did in my 40s. And earning a lot more than I ever have. No wasting time in prayers, temple-going, looking after grandchildren or taking my walking stick for an airing in the park. I can understand that really old people (I would put the minimum qualifying age at 80), who have no one to look after them, or are sick or senile, should be provided accommodation in old people's homes. But others have no business to be doing nothing besides watching TV or boring their friends with stories of their past days—that is unpardonable anecdotage. This kind of defeatism is best left to poets:

Na poochh kaun hain, kyon raah
mein laachaar baithey hain

Musafir hain, safar karney kee
tamanna haar baithey hain.

(Don't ask me who I am, why I sit
helplessly by the roadside;
I am a traveller who has lost the
will to go to my destination.)

Don't hark back to the days of your youth. You will never be
able to recapture them or do what you did in younger days.
That can be self-defeating and frustrating.

Javaanee jaatee rahee, aur hamen
pataa na chalaa
Isee ko dhoond rahey hain, kamar
jhukaye hooey.

(Youth has vanished, and I never
got to know about it,
I keep looking for it with my back
doubled with age.)

In my third year as editor of *The Hindustan Times*, when my
contract was due for renewal, my *anndaataa* (provider) K.K.
Birla asked me, 'Sardar Sahib, *aap ka retire honey kaa vichaar
naheen*—aren't you thinking of retiring?' I was then 69. I
replied, '*Birlaji, retire to main Nigambodh Ghaat mein hoonga*
(I will retire when I am taken to the cremation ground).'

Actually, I plan to be buried so that my rotten guts can
enrich the soil of my motherland after I have gone.

DEATH AS A HOUSEGUEST

'I have had death staying with me for nine years,' he said with a wistful smile. This was former Prime Minister V.P. Singh. We were sitting in my backyard garden. Bright sunshine, balmy autumn air fragrant with aroma of ripening grapefruit, barbets calling, three kittens engaged in mock battles pouncing on each other's tails. God was in his heaven and all was right with the world.

'Do you believe in God?' I asked him.

'I do not,' he replied categorically. 'I find the concept of anyone being almighty unacceptable in a democratic society. Nobody is more powerful than another; all are equal.'

V.P. Singh has had blood cancer and cancer of the bone marrow for the last nine years; his kidneys are impaired. He has to undergo blood transfusion every seven days. He recited a poem:

Every week I ask her (death): is it time for you to take me along?' She replies, 'Nahin, abhee nahin—no, not yet.'

I countered it with my favourite quotation from Allama Iqbal:

Baagh-e-bahisht say mujhay, hukm-e-safar diya thha kyon?
Kaar-e-Jahaan daraaz hai, ab meyra intazaar kar.

(Why did you order me out of the garden of paradise?

I have a lot of work that remains unfulfilled; now you better wait for me.)

V.P. Singh responded: 'Wah! Wah!'

I continued: 'When I feel my end is near, I tell the Badey Mian up in the clouds, "Mian Sahib, I will come to you when I have *fursat* (spare time)." '

Singh nodded his head in approval.

'Do you pray?' I asked him.

'Never,' he replied emphatically. Then corrected himself, 'I did once when my mother was on her deathbed. I prayed to God to spare her. Her condition improved and she survived another two years. But I have never prayed for myself. To me it sounds like *saudey baazee* (barter)—I will sing your praises if you promise me money, success, good health, etc.'

I noticed a gold ring with a lapis lazuli stone in it. 'Why do you wear that good luck charm?' I asked. He took it off and replied, 'My son gave it to me. I wear it when he is around.' From under his shirt he pulled out a necklace. It had a rudraksh bead encrusted in a gold ring. 'I wear this because Ajeet had it made for me to ward off evil.' Ajeet Caur, who had accompanied him, beamed a happy smile. Our dialogue about death was over.

EXPERIENCE OF DEATH

There is sizeable literature on the experiences of people who were declared medically dead, i.e., their hearts had stopped beating but were revived within a few minutes. Most talk of being able to hear their relatives crying over them, dazzling lights and soft music. Sceptics dismiss these experiences as pre-conditional hangovers common to people who believe in God, heaven, hell and the afterlife. None of these beliefs applies to Professor A.J. Ayer who was declared dead but whose heart began to beat again after four minutes. He had published his 'postmortem' experiences in a series of articles.

First let me introduce you to Ayer who did me the honour of dining in my home about 30 years ago. Sir Alfred Julius Ayer (born 1910) was educated at Eton and Christ Church College, Oxford. He became a professor of Logic and taught at various prestigious universities including his *alma mater*. He made his name in 1936 with the publication of *Language, Truth and Logic* as an exponent of logical positivism. His other works include *The Foundations of Empirical Knowledge* (1940) and *The Problem of Knowledge* (1956). Ayer is recognized as England's foremost freethinker and agnostic.

When he 'died' two months ago and came back to life four minutes later, he recorded his experience in an article entitled 'The Undiscovered Country'. He admitted that 'my recent experiences have slightly weakened my conviction that my genuine death will be the end of me.' In a later article he somewhat qualified his belief in the full-stop theory of death saying, 'My experiences have weakened, not my belief that there is no life after death, but my inflexible attitude towards that belief.'

Did Ayer really die and get to 'the other side'? Doctors attending on him hold that although his heart had stopped beating, his brain continued to function. But they added that as soon as the heart stops beating, the brain functioning goes into rapid decline and comes to a halt within four minutes. Ayer's post-mortem experiences were, at best, recollections of an impaired brain.

Ayer summarily dismisses the Judeo-Christian-Muslim belief in the resurrection of the body. None of them tell us in what form the dead will be resurrected—as they were when they died or as young people in good health? What about the ones who die in infancy, cripples and those born mentally challenged? Will we be reborn in the same sex? Will we carry memories of our present lives in our future lives?

Ayer is equally dismissive of the reincarnation theory to which Hindus, Jains, Buddhists and Sikhs subscribe. However, he concedes that if there comes a time when people can really recall experiences of prior lives in greater abundance than hitherto provided, there may be cases for 'licensing re-incarnation'. So far it is no better than science fiction.

LEARNING FROM THE DEAD

Cemeteries have long been my favourite places of recreation. I wouldn't be seen dead in one at night because I have this mortal dread of ghosts. But on a bright, sunny day, I'd rather take a stroll through a cemetery than through any well-laid park or garden. For one, there are not many people living who share my enthusiasm; for another, seeing the hundreds that I have outlasted lying at my feet gives me a sense of having triumphed over them. I read their epitaphs and murmur to myself, 'Poor sod! Born after me; gone before me.' And then I go on to read the next tombstone.

In Washington I was lucky enough to have an apartment close to Arlington cemetery, the largest in the country spreading over hundreds of acres—a green hillside dipping into the Potomac River. Every Sunday morning, hail, rain or snow, I found myself striding along furlong after furlong of tombstones. Since Arlington is primarily meant to house remains of those who fell in battle and their wives, most graves bear only names, dates of birth and demise of their tenants. Only old graves have epitaphs eulogizing the wordly greatness of their occupants. Quite a few Presidents of the United States are buried in Arlington. I was surprised to learn how many had come to a violent end. Of these, the most celebrated was John F. Kennedy, whose grave on the top of the hill is Arlington's chief attraction.

Busloads of tourists come from all parts of the world to have themselves photographed by the flame which burns round the clock and read the many inspiring messages he delivered which are inscribed in a stone round a small amphitheatre. Besides the Kennedy mystique that makes this a hallowed spot, it is the panoramic view it commands that attracts crowds. You get an uninterrupted view of the Potomac from the northern to the southern horizon, and across the river, the Kennedy Centre and the Lincoln and Washington memorials right up to Capitol Hill. On a clear day it is a grand spectacle.

Americans, though they are big on flag waving (Stars and Stripes banners are displayed on most big buildings), do not indulge in hero-worship as much as we do. On the contrary, exploring the seamier, sexier sides of political leaders, captains of industry and celebrities is a national pastime. On the many mornings I was at Kennedy's grave, I rarely met an American, whereas Russians, Chinese, Japanese and Indians came by the busload.

The crest of Arlington cemetery is older and its graves more ornate with the usual paraphernalia of angels, quotes from the Bible and eulogies for the dead. Also, many graves are mounted with equestrian statues.

My friend Orekhov of the Soviet embassy pointed them out to me and asked, 'Do you know that when a horse has one of its legs raised, it means that he fell in the field of battle?'

'The horse or the rider.' I asked.

'Not the horse, the man riding it. It is a well-established statutory convention observed in Europe and North America.'

I bet you didn't know that. We do not observe this convention. Most of our Shivaji statues have his horse with one foreleg raised. He did not die in battle. Those justified in having them would be warriors like Tipu Sultan and Rani Lakshmibai of Jhansi.

LIFE AFTER DEATH

Dr Satya Vrat Shastri, Professor of Sanskrit at Delhi University, returned from a lecture tour of Europe and North America to hear the announcement of an award of Rs. 25,000 from the Sanskrit Akademi of Uttar Pradesh.

Amongst the many topics lectured on was the concept of death in the *Upanishads*. He tells me that in Italy his audience included doctors of medicine, and scientists. They were impressed by what he had to say. I can well understand it because to intelligent Westerners brought up on Hebraic, Christian and Islamic beliefs, the Hindu-Jain-Buddhist-Sikh concept of *Samsara*—birth, death and rebirth—appears altogether more sophisticated than their theories of the Day of Judgement, heaven and hell.

The question remains unanswered: Is there any rational basis for believing that there is life after death? Our scriptures (Hindu, Jain, Buddhist and Sikh) state categorically that there is. Most of this belief is taken from the *Upanishads* and summarized in the *Gita*. It is maintained that on death, the body dies but the soul lives on. The soul changes bodies as a person changes his or her clothes. The *Kathopanishad* asserts that birth, decay and death occur only to the material body but there is something beyond the body which does not perish. It is the *atman* hidden in the heart's cavity.

'Every seventh year all the particles of the body change and get renewed but still one is the same person; the identity never changes.'

The question is, what is the foundation of this identity? Shastri ji answers, 'It means the unchangeable something within beings which is the source of intelligence and existence and upon which our relative existence depends. The *atman* or the permanent entity is birthless...and deathless.'

What exactly *atman* is remains shrouded in mystery, answered by the negative, not this, not that. It is the all-pervasive *parmatma* as well as the individual *jivatman*. When the latter merges into the former, *jyoti jyot milay*—your light mingles with eternal light (*Adi grantha*), and a person achieves liberation (*moksha*) from the cycle of birth, death and rebirth.

At the same time, our Hindu theology also provides a system of reward and punishment through the theory of transmigration of souls as well as interregnum—the state of limbo in which the soul subsists awaiting decision whether to be reborn as a good person for good deeds or as vermin as punishment for evil acts in the previous life.

'*Naisa tarkana matir apaneya* (by argument one cannot explain what survives death),' concedes Dr Shastri. 'There cannot be any scientific proof that *atman* exists after death, it is ever present in the sense that it cannot be verified.'

So why labour with argument: those who believe will go on believing, those who don't are not likely to be converted by jugglery of beautiful phrases. As far as I am concerned, death remains the final full stop. I am, however, more than eager to unravel its mystery and join believers in the prayer:

Asato ma sad gamaya
Tamaso ma jyotir gamaya
Mrtyor ma amrtam gamaya.

(Lead me from unreality to reality
Lead me from darkness to light
Lead me from death to immortality.)

COPING WITH THE DEATH OF A LOVED ONE

There are two schools of thought on the subject—Eastern and Western. Orientals believe that the best way of coping with the death of a loved one like a parent, spouse or child is to cry your heart out till you are drained of tears. The custom *vain* (chants of lament) and breast-beating were regarded as cathartic. All this is followed by *chautha, chaleesveen, bhog, antim ardas* or a prayer meeting in memory of the departed soul. Friends are expected to call in the belief that grief shared is grief halved. Westerners believe that grief is a private matter and should not be exhibited in public. Shedding tears is unmanly. One should put a stoic front and get over the shock of loss by oneself.

I had to cope with the problem myself very recently. Being an agnostic, I could not find solace in religious rituals. Being essentially a loner, I discouraged friends and relations coming to condole with me on the death of my wife. Most of them ignored my request and came to see me. I found this commiserating with me on my emotional trauma. I spent the first night alone sitting in my chair in the dark. At times I broke down, but soon recovered my composure. A couple of days later, I resumed my usual routine of work from dawn to dusk. That took my mind off the stark reality of having to live alone in an empty home for the rest of my days. But friends persisted on calling, and upsetting my equilibrium. So I packed myself off to Goa to be alone by myself. I was not sure if it would work out.

Everyone has to evolve his or her own formula of coping with grief. People who believe in God turn to Him. Words of the 34th Psalm are pertinent: 'The Lord is close to the broken-hearted and saves those who are crushed in spirit.' Jesus Christ who was an Oriental was not ashamed of weeping before everyone when he lost a friend. So it is recorded in the Bible (John 11-33-38): 'When Jesus saw many weeping and the Jews who had come along with him also weeping, he was deeply marred in spirit and troubled: "Where have you laid him?" he asked. "Come and see Lord," they replied. Jesus wept. Then the Jews said, "See how he loved him!"'

As one would expect, Osho Rajneesh made light of the darkest of subjects, including ways of coping with grief. In his collection of sermons *Walking in Zen, Sitting in Zen*, he cites the case of an Italian, Perelli, and his method of getting over the shock of losing his wife: 'At the funeral of his wife, Perelli made a terrible scene, so terrible and heart-rending, in fact, that friends had to forcibly restrain him from jumping into the grave and being buried with his beloved Maria. Then, still overcome with grief, he was taken home in the rented limousine and immediately went into complete seclusion.

'A week passed and nothing was heard of him. Finally, worried about the poor guy, his late wife's brother went to the house. After ringing the doorbell for ten minutes—and still worried—the brother-in-law jimmied the front door, went upstairs and found his dead sister's husband busy with the maid.'

'The bedroom was a mess—empty champagne bottles everywhere. "This is terrible, Perelli!" the brother-in-law declared in shocked tones. "Your dead wife, my sister, has been dead only a week and you're doing this! You're doing this!" So busy was Perelli that he managed only to turn his head. "How do I know what I'm doing?" he said. "I got such grief! I got such grief!" '

At one time Jains, Hindus and Sikhs celebrated the passing of the elders who had led a full life. They decorated their biers with balloons and buntings, and funeral processions were led by brass bands playing military marches or films songs right from their homes to cremation grounds. It is a pity that not many today follow this custom. The death of aged people, particularly those who died after prolonged illnesses, should be looked upon as a reprieve from suffering, and celebrated.

Part 2

AFTER LIFE

Z.A. BHUTTO: FROM THE DEATH
SENTENCE TO THE GALLOWS

For the last two days that I have been in Islamabad and
Rawalpindi, an unseasonal rain has been lashing the cities,
and chill wind has been blowing from cloud-covered Marghala
Hills. Nevertheless, people were out in the cold rain to cluster
around news stalls to scan the latest supplements of Urdu
papers.

When the first intimation that Bhutto would be hanged on
the morning of 4 April appeared, I was in the Sadar Bazaar.
Copies of *Dadagat* were quickly sold out and read in silence by
groups. Some shed tears, some sighed, but no voices were
raised. There were armed policemen and units of the army all
over the bazaar breathing down the necks of citizens
everywhere. Although a pall of gloom spread over the city,
there was no fear of violence from the soldiers or the
policemen. They seemed to share the apprehensions of the
people over the uncertain future of their country.

The people had reconciled themselves to the idea of
Bhutto being hanged. Whatever support there was for him and
resentment against the present regime was muted. Most of

Bhutto's supporters are in detention. No reliable figures are available, but upwards of 25,000 are known to be held all over the country. The figure may well be four times that. Mr. Abdul Hafeez Pirzada, who was Law Minister in Bhutto's cabinet, put the figure as high as 200,000. It is evident that though the administration is loath to take action immediately, it is determined to crush the slightest manifestation of protest if that protest threatens to assume the proportions of a mass movement. Protests there certainly will be, but they will be delayed and probably surface nearer the time of the general election promised next November.

There is a curious paradox in the Pakistan political scene. Most people concede that if Bhutto had been let out of gaol and there were to be a free and fair election today, his party would sweep the polls. At the same time, political analysts concede that there is little likelihood of a spontaneous rising in favour of Bhutto. The paradox is explained thus: Bhutto was undoubtedly very popular amongst the masses because of the populist slogans he had coined and the promises he had made to them: freedom from hunger (roti), a change of clothes (kapda) and a roof over their heads (makaan). They knew that he had neither the intention nor the means to fulfil these promises, but to the hungry, hate-fed, homeless millions, the mirage was better than nothing.

'What did Bhutto give you?' asked an irate anti-Bhutto politician of a rabble of landless peasantry (kammis). Prompt came the reply: 'Even if he did not give us what he promised, he gave us zabaan (tongue) to ask for our rights.'

It was Bhutto who coined the word istisaal (from the Arabic for 'exploitation') and told workers in factories that they were being exploited by landlords and common soldiers, that their officers were misusing them.

'Do not suffer istisaal any more; I will put an end to it,' he had promised.

Most people did not understand what the word *istisaal* meant except that it connoted something that they could do without. Bhutto also enjoyed the reputation of being a clever man, smarter than any other politician in the land and perhaps the only one who could talk on the level with the wiliest of the world's statesmen. It did not bother the people very much that Bhutto was himself a *wadhero* (landlord) given to rich living. What if he had several wives and a mistress or two! What if he was occasionally drunk, used bawdy language and filthy abuse, or had a few people bumped off, beaten or put behind bars? Most heads of state are known to do that and get away with it. To them the only mistake Bhutto committed was to leave a trail of clues of a crime and allow himself to get caught.

The view of Bhutto was not shared by the educated, urban elite of Pakistan who recall his years of misrule during which many opposition politicians were murdered, their families, including their womenfolk, insulted, and thousands of innocent men and women put behind bars. The people of Pakistan came to be sharply divided in their attitude towards Bhutto. Some continued to worship him, others to loathe him. A lady whose husband had been beaten up and imprisoned by Bhutto exploded in anger and said to me, 'I could hang him with my own hands; I would hang him ten times over.' What was needed was the healing touch. The only person who could have given this was President Zia-ul Haq. But ever since the last day for filing petitions for mercy passed without any of Bhutto's wives or children begging for his life, the feeling grew that President Zia had been deprived of the option of granting clemency and had lost the chance of providing the healing touch.

Mr. Abdul Hafeez Pirzada (Bhutto's Law Minister) and Mr. Aziz Ahmed (Bhutto's Foreign Minister) did plead for Bhutto's life. Also, the four other men convicted with him begged for mercy on the grounds that they had no personal animus against Ahmed Raza Kasuri or his father and were only carrying out the orders of Bhutto. Rabia Khanam, mother of Arshad Iqbal, one of the condemned men, denounced Bhutto as a 'cruel dictator whom no one could dare to disobey'. What probably persuaded President Zia-ul Haq to go ahead with the execution was the sort of reasoning put forward by Mr. Ahmed Raza Kasuri, the 'marked man', whom the assassins failed to kill and slew his father instead. In a Press interview, Mr. Ahmed Raza Kasuri stated that Bhutto alive will 'be a constant danger' to Pakistan and if he is not hanged, his (Kasuri's) mother will demonstrate before the President's house. Mr. Kasuri said that if Bhutto's sentence was commuted to life imprisonment or remitted, he would pose a constant danger to the country; if released under political pressure, he would play a devilish role from outside. Bhutto himself knew no mercy, the word was not found in his dictionary, so he deserved none himself. The same sentiment was expressed by some theologians, notably Maulana Mohammed Hussaini Hazari, Senior Vice-President of the Ulema Council of the Pakistan National Alliance. The Maulana described Bhutto as 'a black spot on the face of humanity' and holds him responsible for the disintegration of the country.

'The affair has dragged on too long,' said a senior official of the Ministry of External Affairs to me. 'It should have been decided one way or the other as soon as the death sentence was confirmed.' The anti-Bhutto elements fully agreed with this and went further to say that if General Zia had shot Bhutto on the night of 5 July 1977 instead of arresting him, he would have spared himself and his country of these months of agony: *Garba kushtan roz-e-avval*—if you wish to kill a kitten, do it on its first day.

The curtain rose for the final act in the drama of Zulfikar Ali Bhutto's life at 8.30 a.m. on 18 March 1978. The scene was the main courtroom of the High Court of Lahore. It is a large hall divided into three by two sets of wooden railings. On the northern end sitting at a higher level were five judges in their wigs and black gowns. Facing them in the main body of the hall were members of the High Court bar including counsels for the prosecution and the defence, likewise attired in black. Behind them separated by another railing were members of the public. And on the western wing, alongside the judges and the lawyers, stood the five accused with armed police escort behind them. Chief amongst them was Zulfikar Ali Bhutto, impeccably dressed in a light spring suit and sporting a tie.

No prior notice had been given of this day of judgement. The lawyers engaged in the case had been rung up by the Registrar in the early hours and asked to be present in the main room. The accused were brought in from the Kot Lakhpat gaol in the Black Maria under heavy escort. Word had however got round and the courtroom was packed.

All eyes were turned on the acting Chief Justice, Mushtaq Hussain. He read a summary of the unanimous verdict of the five judges in the case of the murder of Nawab Mohammed Raza Kasuri on the night of November 10-11, 1974 at Lahore. All the accused had pleaded not guilty. Four had presented their defence. Only one, Zulfikar Ali Bhutto, had refused to take part in the proceedings.

Justice Mushtaq Hussain finished reading the findings of the panel of judges and proceeded to pass the sentence: 'To be hanged by the neck till you are dead.'

All eyes turned from the judges to the accused, mainly to Zulfikar Ali Bhutto. He heard the sentence without flinching and simply turned his face away from the judges. He was lost in his own thoughts. 'You could see that he was stunned,' said one of the lawyers. 'But he showed no sign of fear or anger, it seemed as if he had not heard the judge. Or believed it was some kind of grim charade he was witnessing.'

There were no slogans of any kind, no expression of approval or disgust. Neither Bhutto's wife Nusrat nor his daughter Benazir were in the court. And armed police were all over the place.

Lawyers representing the four other accused went over to them for consultation; Bhutto having boycotted the High Court proceedings had no one to talk to him and remained lost in himself for sometime.

Back in the Kot Lakhpat gaol, six rooms had been reserved for Bhutto. He went straight to his room and flopped on the bed fully dressed. He had his eyes fixed on the ceiling. 'He lay there for an hour or more without moving,' says a warder. 'Only when I approached him and asked him if he would like to eat something, I noticed he had been crying. He did not answer me.'

At 11 a.m. the lawyer, Mr Yahya Bakhtiar, came to visit him. The two men embraced each other and broke down: 'Is this the end?' asked Bhutto. 'No,' replied Bakhtiar emphatically. 'We shall appeal against the sentence.' They talked for quite some time. Bhutto's spirits were revived and he was more himself.

According to gaol rules, prisoners condemned to death have to be lodged in specially designed cells, on which constant watch can be maintained to prevent inmates from taking their own lives. Only in the morning and evening are they let out for half-an-hour to take exercise or *tehlaee*.

At 5 a.m. Bhutto was removed to a condemned cell but at his insistence he was allowed to wear his own clothes, keep his own bed, chair and eat his own food. He was given writing material and got all the magazines and newspapers he desired. The mood of depression descended on him again and according to a jail warder, 'He lay on his bed like a dead rat.' This lasted for a couple of days.

It seems that the appeals of clemency from different heads of state published in the papers revived his sagging spirits. He began to believe that the chorus of protests from all parts of the world would deter the courts and rulers of Pakistan from doing him harm and all the exercise was to break his morale. He resolved to show no sign of cracking under the strain.

Yahya Bakhtiar filed the appeal in the Supreme Court. Since the court was located in Rawalpindi, in mid-May Bhutto and his co-accused were transferred to the gaol in Rawalpindi—ironically alongside the very mansion from which only a few months earlier he had ruled Pakistan. A set of four rooms normally reserved for women convicted of murder, were prepared for him. He had a bedroom, a study, a bathroom and a kitchen all to himself. Once again gaol regulations were overlooked in order to make the distinguished prisoner comfortable. He was given a *niwaar* (canvas) bed instead of a hospital-type steel bed, a rubber foam mattress, his own blankets, fan and light with the switchboard within his reach. He was also furnished with a table, chair, table lamp, books and magazines. His food and his Havana cigars came from his home. He wore his own clothes (he had two suitcases full of them) and used his own shaving kit. He was allowed an hour everyday with his counsel and could take his half hour of *tehlaee* at times of his own choosing. Since winters in Rawalpindi are sharp, he was provided with electric heaters. His wife and daughter joined him for tea in the afternoon. Very often, Benazir lay on the same bed with her father and the two talked in whispers to avoid being overheard by the ever-present warders and to ensure their dialogue was not recorded by bugging devices.

On 6 February 1979, the Supreme Court dismissed Bhutto's appeal. He was not present in court. The news was conveyed by the gaol superintendent. His only comment was; 'This is very sad,' followed by a question, 'Was it unanimous?' The superintendent, without checking, replied, 'Yes.' Bhutto remarked, 'That is very surprising.'

When the news reached Nusrat Bhutto at Sihala (15 miles from Pindi) where she was under house arrest, she got into a car, broke through the police cordon and stormed up to the gaol gates. She was allowed to meet her husband. She collapsed in his arms. When she came to, the first question he asked her was, 'Was it unanimous?' Nusrat told him that of the seven judges of the Supreme Court three had given him the benefit of the doubt. 'Don't worry!' he assured her. 'We will go in for a review.'

Once the death sentence had been confirmed, the gaol authorities decided to treat Bhutto as they treated other convicts under sentence of death. They took away his shaving kit, removed the *niwaar* bed (*niwaar* can be used to hang oneself) and stopped home food. Bhutto refused to lie in the hospital bed. Instead, he spread the rubber foam mattress on the floor; it was to be his bed till his last day. By the afternoon, the government relented and let him have home-cooked food.

On 24 March 1979, the Supreme Court rejected the review petition. The last ray of hope was extinguished. Yahya Bakhtiar's role as Bhutto's lawyer was over, but he requested the court to let him see Bhutto. The prosecution represented by M.A. Rahman made no objection. Out the court room Yahya Bakhtiar told waiting pressmen that there were grounds for a second review petition. Meanwhile, the superintendent of the gaol wrote a formal memorandum to Bhutto informing him of the confirmation of the death sentence and telling him that he had seven days to make a petition for mercy. When he took it to Bhutto and asked him to sign on the carbon copy, he refused to do so and dismissed him brusquely, 'Yes, yes, I know all about it.'

The next day (25 March 1979) the Lahore High Court issued a 'Black' warrant to the five convicted men specifying that they were liable to be executed after 4 April 1979. The exact date was kept a secret.

Bhutto was allowed to receive as many relatives and friends as he wished. His first wife, Ameer Begum, uncles, cousins, including Mumtaz Bhutto, an erstwhile Cabinet colleague, Hafeez Pirzada, were amongst the many who came to see him. All visitors were searched and no one was allowed inside the cell; a six-foot-wide table was placed in front of the iron grill to prevent physical contact (or passing of cyanide or other poison).

One night Bhutto sent for the deputy superintendent of the gaol and asked him to send for Hafeez Pirzada. Bhutto made no specific request to Pirzada to appeal for mercy but the words he used were 'Marna bahut mushkil hota hai' (dying is not easy), and the fact that Pirzada did in fact file a petition after his last meeting on 1 April 1979 indicates that Bhutto, without relenting from his determination never to beg for his life, still hoped that somehow, someone would make General Zia hold his hand. While leaving the jail, Pirzada was asked by pressmen whether Bhutto had made an appeal for mercy. He replied, 'No, he has not. But I will do so.'

Pirzada appealed to President Zia to spare Bhutto's life. His appeal was widely published but there was no comment from the President's office.

The decision to execute Bhutto on 4 April was taken two days earlier (2 April). Rules required executions to take place at 5.30 a.m. (or 6 a.m. in winter)—but the hour was fixed at 2 a.m. to avoid demonstrations and give time to have the body flown to Larkana and interred in the family graveyard in village Nao Dero. Meanwhile, the hangman, Tara Masih, was brought from Bahawalpur to Lahore. There was speculation that the condemned man might be taken to the Kot Lakhpat gaol to be executed.

On 3 April 1979, Nusrat and Benazir Bhutto were brought from Sihala to Rawalpindi jail at 11 a.m. They demanded to be told whether or not this was to be their last meeting. They received an evasive reply: *'Aap yeh hee samajh len* (you may take it as so).' When the wife and daughter told Bhutto of it, he sent for the gaol superintendent and received confirmation that as far as *mulakaats* (meetings) were concerned this was to be the *aakhree* (last). The exact hour when the hanging would take place was not divulged.

Nusrat and Benazir spent three hours with Bhutto talking across the table. For once Bhutto was indiscreet and gave instructions about some papers which he had secreted away behind the walls in his Larkana house. Within four hours the house was searched and the papers were recovered.

There are heart-rending accounts of this last meeting between Bhutto and his wife and daughter. Benazir's request to let her embrace her father or at least touch his feet before going was firmly turned down. A silver salver in which tea was served to Bhutto was handed back to her with the words *'Ab Sahib ko iskee zaroorat nahin padegee* (the Sahib will not need this anymore).' It was obvious that the hour of doom was near. Nusrat and Benazir left the jail around 2.30 p.m. and demanded to be taken to see President Zia-ul Haq. The superintendent rang up the President's house and was told to tell the ladies to put whatever they wanted to say on paper.

At 4 p.m. a magistrate arrived with writing material and asked Bhutto to write his last will which he would attest for him. Bhutto spent an hour or more writing out his last message. No one will ever know what he wrote because with his own cigar lighter he burnt the paper to ashes.

At 6 p.m. he asked for hot water and his shaving set saying, 'I don't want to die looking like a mullah.' And after he had erased the growth on his chin, he looked into the mirror and remarked in self-mockery, 'Now I look like a third world leader.'

A maulvi arrived with a *tasbih* (rosary) and *musalla* (prayer mat) to assist Bhutto in his last prayers. Bhutto put the rosary round his neck but told the maulvi to remove the prayer mat and himself as he did not need anyone's assistance to meet his Maker.

Then the bravado went out of him. He lay down on the mattress and went into a kind of coma. As the time of execution drew near, other inmates of the jail were woken up and ordered to chant verses from the holy *Koran*. Only Bhutto remained impervious to the goings-on. At 1.30 a.m. jail officials accompanied by a magistrate and doctor arrived to take him out on his last journey to the scaffold. The superintendent shook him and said: '*Bhutto Sahib, jaaney ka waqt aa gayaa hai*' (It is time to go).

There are different versions of what followed. According to one, Bhutto woke up and as soon as he saw the men with handcuffs, he panicked. He tried various ploys to play for time: he wanted to take a bath, write his will, have a cup of tea. But all were firmly but politely denied to him. According to the second version, he refused to be woken up. The superintendent feared that he had taken his own life and sent for the doctor. The doctor felt his pulse, heard his heartbeat through his stethoscope and opened his eyelids to make sure that he was alive. In either case, he was unable or unwilling to get up and had to be put on a stretcher. Since he was supine his hands were cuffed in front instead of behind him as prescribed for condemned men on their last journey.

Extensive precautions had been taken against possible attempts to storm the gaol: names of the PLO and even some foreign governments were whispered as likely to make a desperate bid to save Bhutto. Precautions taken included lookouts for parachutists and hostile helicopters. Consequently, a very large number of defence personnel were present in the gaol at the time. it is estimated that upward of 250 men saw the execution with their own eyes.

The scaffold is quite a distance from the condemned cell.

The party with Bhutto on the stretcher arrived at the foot of the gallows at about 1.45 a.m. As the stretcher was put down and the superintendent approached Bhutto, he suddenly sat up. He mumbled some words which were interpreted as 'Nusrat will be left alone.' When the handcuffs were unlocked and his hands tied behind him, he is reported to have protested that the knot was too tight. Then without assistance he went up the steps to the gallows. Before Tara Masih put the black hood over his face, Bhutto's lips moved. According to one version, he mumbled, 'Finish it!' According to another his lips moved but no sound came from them.

The trap was sprung exactly at 2 a.m. and the dapper, flamboyant Zulfikar, once President and Prime Minister of Pakistan, and next to Jinnah, its most popular leader, (*Quaid-i-Awaam*) plunged to his doom.

At the time of death, Bhutto was dressed in salwaar-kameez which he had elevated to the status of an *awaami* suit. He had a gold Zenith watch on his wrist and a gold ring with three diamonds on his finger. After Hayat Mohammed, a humble servitor in a Pindi mosque, had bathed his corpse and draped it in a shroud, somebody noticed that the diamond-studded ring was missing. The superintendent immediately arrested Tara Masih and Hayat Mohammed and ordered them to be searched. The ring was found in the pocket of the hangman, Tara Masih. Both the watch and the ring were handed over to Benazir Bhutto the next morning.

The body was flown to Larkana and then taken to Nao Dero. Bhutto's first wife, Ameer Begum, 15 years older than him, his uncles, aunts and other relatives were allowed to see the dead man's face. It was serene and calm as if in deep slumber with no visible marks of injury save a gash in the neck. (There is no truth in the story that men who are hanged have their necks elongated and their eyes and tongues hang out.)

Bhutto's execution will wipe out memories of his evil deeds

and highlight some of the good he did for his country. He is already being acclaimed as a martyr. There are reports of people going to his grave to offer *fateha* (prayer) for the peace of his soul. Many are reported to kiss the grave, pick the dust about the grave and smear it on their foreheads. In every hamlet, village, town and city stretching from the Khyber to Karachi groups gather to offer *ghaibana Namaz-e-Janaaza* (funeral prayers in the absence of the body). Bhutto's ghost has already emerged from its tomb; it will not be long before it turns the illusory dreams of power of the ruling generals into a nightmare.

The beneficiaries of Bhutto's 'martyrdom', as it will inevitably be described in times to come, will be the top leaders of the PPP including his cousin, Mumtaz Ali Bhutto, Mr Abdul Hafeez Pirzada, General Tikka Khan, who is held in great esteem in Pakistan, and above all his daughter, Benazir Bhutto.

SANJAY GANDHI: YOUNG DICTATOR

It was a hot sweltering afternoon in June 1980, when neither man nor beast stirred out of the shade. And there was I, standing under a scorching sun amidst a sweaty crowd on the roundabout near India Gate. I wanted to say my last farewell to my young friend as he passed by. I recalled that sixteen years ago I had stood at the same spot in the same kind of torrid heat to watch the cortège of my friend's grandsire. His grandsire had been a national figure for more than half a century and then Prime Minister for seventeen years. There had been elaborate *bandobast* (arrangements) for his funeral. My young friend was a political *parvenue* who had been villified and slandered from the day he became a major, persecuted and gaoled off and on and had only recently managed to get into Parliament. Yet the crowd at his funeral was larger than the one I had seen at his grandsire's. Someone had quoted an apt couplet in Urdu:

Ai gulcheen-e-ajal tujh sey nadaani hooe
phool voh tora ke gulshan men veeranee hooee.

(O thou picker of life's flowers; you made a grave mistake; You plucked the one flower which laid the garden desolate.)

The cortège came along led by bands of young men canting:

Jab tak sooraj chaand rahega
Sanjay tera naam rahega.

(As long as the sun and moon go round, Sanjay will thy name resound.)

Back home I pondered over this strange phenomenon. The only explanation I could find was that in the last year or two of his life, unnoticed by anyone, a Sanjay cult had grown.

It was very much like the cult of Che Guevara based on the worship of a man who lived dangerously, cocked a snook at convention and tradition, was more feared than loved, and above all feared nothing himself. All these applied to Sanjay. I recall him saying that a leader who is feared is more respected than a leader who is loved. 'That's why when I tell them to do something, they damn well do it.'

Who will now become the leader of the Sanjayists? I don't see the mantle drop on the shoulders of his brother, Rajiv. He is too withdrawn, unambitious, and a man of the family. Nor on Kamal Nath or Jagdish Tytler or the young Scindia. None of them has the derring-do or the panache that was associated with Sanjay. The only possible inheritor of the cult figure is Maneka. She is like her late husband, utterly fearless. And when roused, the very reincarnation of Durga astride a tiger.

TIKKA KHAN: 'BUTCHER OF BANGLADESH'

The name may have faded from the memories of most Indians but will remain tattooed in red in the minds of our Bangladeshi neighbours. He was sent out by General Yahya Khan of Pakistan to put down unrest swelling in East Pakistan. He did it in the only way he knew: let loose his predominantly Punjabi army on hapless Bangladeshis with permission to loot, rape and kill anyone it suspected of being disloyal to Pakistan. His tenure in Dhaka was extensively covered by the world media. He was dubbed the Butcher of Bangladesh. He died in Islamabad on 28 March 2002, at the age of 86.

After Bangladesh won its independence, I went to Pakistan on the invitation of its new ruler Zulfikar Ali Bhutto. I was anxious to meet (by then retired) General Tikka Khan to get his side of the story. He turned down my request for an interview. He did not want to see any Indian, least of all a Sikh journalist. I asked my friend Manzur Qadir to plead on my behalf. He assured General Tikka Khan that I bore no ill will towards Pakistan and I would faithfully report what he had to say about his role in the uprising in what was to become Bangladesh.

It turned out to be quite a memorable interview. General Tikka Khan received me in his bungalow. I was surprised how unmartial he looked—more like a bank clerk than a soldier. He was short and stocky. Also gruff. With him in the room where we sat was his orderly, a huge Pathan about 6 feet 6 inches tall, but gentle as a lamb. I looked around the room cluttered with family photographs and trophies one sees in homes of senior army officers. On the walls were quotations from the *Koran,* including one I could recognize prominently displayed on the mantelpiece.

The General was a very angry man. His *gussa* (anger) was directed entirely against Indians, not against Bangladeshis. Words like *daghaa* (treachery), *dhokaa* (double-dealing), *jhoot* (lies) flowed like lava out of a volcano. He claimed that the sobriquet Butcher of Bangladesh was coined by the Indian media.

'We are god-fearing Muslims,' he repeated over and over again. 'Our soldiers are disciplined and do not indulge in rape and violence against innocent women.'

I let him have his say and asked him as gently as I could, 'Why had the Pakistani army done so poorly against the Indians?'

'*Daghaa,*' he repeated. 'The Indian Army had infiltrated into East Pakistan long before we were forced to declare war.'

I pointed out that there had hardly been any pitched battles. Wherever Indians came against resistance, they avoided fighting and let the Mukti Bahini keep the Pakistanis hemmed in their pockets.

The General's orderly who had seen the action blurted out: '*Awaam hamaaray khilaaf thaa* (the people had turned against us).'

The General did not like his orderly speaking out of turn and snubbed him. I pressed the point home: 'General Sahib, there must have been reason for the common people to turn against you.'

He parried my suggestion and repeated it was all Indian propaganda. I let him have his say. Before taking leave I pointed out to the quotation from the *Koran* embellishing his mantelpiece. He read it out boldly in Arabic: '*Nasr min Allah, fateh un qareeb* (Allah grants victory to the side whose cause is just).'

'General Sahib, Allah granted victory to us Indians.'

He felt I had hit him below the belt. 'Sardar Sahib, I suspect you knew the quotation from the holy book.'

I nodded my head, shook his hand and took my leave.

M.O. MATHAI: NEHRU'S NEMESIS

Although I do not subscribe to the sentiment that one should not speak ill of the dead, I am not going to say anything against Mathai but against the institution of what may best be described as Mathaism. Before I do that I should refresh your memory about this man Mathai who died recently. Till 1952 no one outside his family and circle of friends had heard of him. He had done some kind of clerical job with the American Army during World War II. In 1946 he attached himself to Jawaharlal Nehru and slowly wormed his way up to gaining his confidence and becoming one of his family. He was made Special Secretary to the Prime Minister. This position not only gave him an insight into the private lives of Jawaharlal Nehru, and Feroze and Indira Gandhi but also gave him enormous power—power without responsibility or accountability to anyone save the PM. To quote his own words: 'No file or paper reached the PM except through me. Nothing went out except through me...officials used to refer to me as Deputy PM... and the power behind the throne.' It is little wonder that he became arrogant: 'Except for a few, I had only contempt for ministers who were nothing but a bunch of mediocrities or worse.' Even Panditji was constrained to record that he was 'a person who often acted foolishly in small matters and sometimes threw his weight about'.

Power corrupted Mathai. He had plenty of opportunity to exploit his position as he boasted: 'I have been instrumental in the appointment of innumerable ministers, governors and non-official ambassadors.' He touched many rich people (including the Birlas) for money for a charitable trust he set up. It is apparent that it was not Mathai's capabilities that had put him in the position he held but the fact that he convinced everyone that he could get Nehru to do anything he wanted. He came in by the backdoor and reigned supreme in Teen Murti House till he was fired in 1959.

It was after Mathai had been stripped of the Nehru feathers that he revealed his truly mean nature and dishonoured the confidence that the Nehru family had reposed in him. Nehru, being a generous man, was willing to forgive and take him back. When this was suggested to Mathai he snarled: 'Only a dog returns to his vomit.'

For eighteen years after his dismissal Mathai chewed the cud of bitterness. After Nehru was dead and Indira Gandhi out of power, Mathai felt safe enough to spew out venom against the family whose salt he had eaten. In his *Reminiscences of the Nehru Age,* published during the Janata regime, he exposed Jawaharlal's affairs with a succession of women, denigrated Feroze Gandhi as something of a nitwit and a philanderer, described Indira not as his wife but a 'concubine' and one vain enough 'to try and put herself two steps higher than her father while she was Prime Minister. Poor fish! I suppose most women are overburdened by illusions.' The most sinister part of the *Reminiscences* was the unpublished Chapter Twenty-Nine entitled 'She' which the publishers with all the sanctimoniousness at their command withheld but not without whetting the readers' prurient appetites by printing:

'This chapter on an intensely personal experience of the author written without inhibition in the D.H. Lawrence style, has been withdrawn by the author at the last moment.' (The reference is obviously to Lawrence's *Lady Chatterly's Lover* which tells of a torrid love affair between the lady of the house and a gamekeeper.)

Mathai is dead. I hope Chapter Twenty-Nine went up in flames with him. But Mathaism is very much alive. One Mathai goes, another takes his place. Wherever there is concentration of power, there are people who manage by assiduous flattery and professions of loyalty to get close to it. By sheer physical proximity they acquire power for themselves and confidential information which helps them to perpetuate their hold: they come to know too much and it becomes hazardous to retire them or to get rid of them. Such men are dangerous.

My belated farewell pronouncement on 'Mac' Mathai is taken from Noel Coward: 'He was a little man, that was his trouble. Never trust a man with short legs; his brains are too close to his bottom.'

MOUNTBATTEN: LORD OF BALONEY

Two brief encounters, one in London followed by another a few months later in Toronto (Canada), have stayed in my mind. At the time I did not have the nerve to put my reactions in print: he was the Lord of Destiny, an awe-inspiring figure of whom singing anything but paeans of praise would have sounded discordant; Ziegler's excellent biography *Mountbatten* assures me that I was not wrong in suspecting that the emperor had no clothes. Or wore a flimsy see-through raiment.

The first meeting was unscheduled. Lord Mountbatten was the chief guest at a reception in India House. By some error he turned up fifteen minutes before he was expected and even the host, Krishna Menon, was not present to receive him. I rushed down to greet him, apologized for the misunderstanding and suggested that he relax in my temporary office which in any case was reserved for his wife and bore the plaque 'Countess Mountbatten of Burma'.

His Lordship was out of countenance. He had come splendidly attired in an Admiral's deep-blue uniform splattered with gold epaulettes, ribbons and a chest full of medals. Instead of making a spectacular entry at a glittering reception as he had planned, he was having to waste time with a nondescript clerical type. I did my best to keep him amused. I asked him about the Partition and the stormy days that followed. He answered me in bored monosyllables. I tried to provoke him: 'Lord Mountbatten, many people feel that if you had not forced the pace, the exchange of populations might have been smoother and we might have been spared the enormous bloodshed that took place.'

He was needled into replying: 'I don't give a damn about what my critics say today,' he said angrily. 'I will be judged at the bar of history.'

I was taken aback by his pomposity. However justified, I did not expect a sophisticated English gentleman of breeding to air assumptions of immortality. It wasn't pukka.

The next encounter revealed another facet of Lord Mountbatten's character. He was to inaugurate an international trade fair in Toronto. Out of the blue we were informed that His Lordship had desired that his escort should be provided by the Indian High Commission in Canada. We were very happy to learn that he had such affection for India that even after laying down office as Viceroy and Governor-General he wanted to perpetuate his Indian connection.

It was a warm, bright summer morning. There was an enormous crowd. He arrived in his Rolls Royce flying the Union Jack. This time he wore a white sharkskin uniform with the same gold and silver tinsel and medallions spread over it. We lined up behind him: two bearded sardars in black *sherwanis* and *chooridars* followed by our army, navy and air force attachés in their respective uniforms. The Canadians went delirious at the sight. This was the British Empire at the zenith of its glory! The tall, splendidly attired White Rajah with his complement of loyal black subjects in attendance. We stood behind him while he spoke. His speech was punctuated with allusions to his royal connection: 'My cousin the King; my nephew the Queen's consort; my uncle the Duke of some place or the other, etc., etc.' It went down beautifully because the *bandobast* (arrangements) was tickety boo—a favourite expression of Lord Mountbatten. The entire tamasha had been masterminded by the greatest political showman of his times.

Was there anything of substance to this man? I am not sure. He was certainly well born: Queen Victoria was present at his christening. He did not have much education; his class of people did not have to bother too much with books. He did not have much money. He made up for these shortcomings by marrying an enormously wealthy, partly Jewish wife. She habitually cuckolded him and he suffered the indignity for the simple reason that he could not afford to live in the style he wanted to without her money. He was a name-dropper who exploited his connections to the fullest extent.

However, there was also a lot to him on the plus side. He was not a snob and was always at ease with hoi polloi. Being of limited vision he could take bold decisions without being unduly concerned with their consequences. I cannot think of another contemporary who owed his rise to eminence largely because he married the right woman and because luck was always on his side. Ziegler is right when he sums up his portrayal in the following words:

> A picture of Mountbatten without his warts would indeed be unconvincing, for, like everything else about him, his faults were on the grandest scale. His vanity, though child-like, was monstrous, his ambition unbridled. The truth, in his hands, was swiftly converted from what it was to what it should have been. He sought to rewrite history with cavalier indifference to the facts to magnify his own achievements. There was a time when I became so enraged by what I began to feel was his determination to hoodwink me that I found it necessary to place on my desk a notice saying, 'Remember, in spite of everything, he was a great man.'

RAJNI PATEL: MARXIST MILLIONAIRE

Why do people take the life out of a full-blooded person when paying him tributes on his demise? Rajni Patel was larger than life itself, packed with ingredients both good and bad which made him the kind of human dynamo he was. But all our wretched politicians and journalists could say about him were cliché-ridden eulogies they spout about every celebrity when he departs: great son of India, freedom fighter, great jurist etc., etc. More than liver cancer or cardiac arrest, it was these banal homilies that killed Rajni after his death.

Rajni had many lovable qualities: the gift of friendship, standing by his friends even when he knew they were in the wrong, princely generosity, love of liquor and beautiful women. He also had many shortcomings: lack of political and financial scruples, preaching what he did not practise and calculated name-dropping. In the half century that I knew him I saw both sides of the Rajni coin. But so strong was his affection for his friends that none of us had the courage to disown him; the best any of us could do was to slowly extricate oneself from his circle.

I first met Rajni when he was at Cambridge University. He was an ardent Communist; I was not. Our dialogues always ended up in a brawl. Once he, Krishna Menon and I had to travel together to Paris. Both ignored my presence throughout the six-hour journey. When I went to live in Bombay, Rajni had ceased being a member of the Communist Party and had joined the Indira Gandhi Congress. 'We are now members of the same church,' he said to me. Thereafter we exchanged hospitality on a weekly basis.

At the time Rajni had broken with his second wife Susheila—a woman of extraordinary beauty; Nordic complexion, Hellenic features and grey-green eyes that most Chitpavan Brahmins have. Their three sons lived with the mother. Rajni had taken up with a Gujarati divorcee, Bakul Bhatt, who was almost twenty years younger than he. Susheila did not forgive him for ditching her and embarrassed him at many public meetings.

Rajni and Bakul were obviously very much in love with each other but it was at a drinking orgy many years later, with Rajni very high in his cups, that at a midnight ceremony, the two were pronounced man and wife.

Rajni's rise to eminence was as spectacular as it was sinister. He had no political base whatsoever: to describe him as a labour leader is absolute hogwash; he could not have won a district board by-election, It was during his tenure as President that the Bombay Pradesh Congress Committee became a kind of board of directors of an affluent company. He was the pioneer in the cult of businessmen-politicians. Rajni's methods of extracting money from the wealthy made his predecessor money-collectors S.K. Patil and Atulya Ghosh appear like novices. I recall one evening when he had invited a bevy of millionaires to raise money to help the drought-stricken in Maharashtra. With Royal Salute Scotch (Rs 1,500 per bottle) and French champagne, we discussed hunger and famine. As usual at every one of Rajni's parties, the discussion was interrupted many times by Bakul announcing that Rajni was wanted on the phone by the Prime Minister or some member of her Cabinet. Those who were there for the first time were very impressed.

However, there is no denying the fact that every person who was anybody sought Rajni's patronage. I cannot count the number of chief ministers, governors, millionaires, generals, admirals and politicians that I met in his apartment.

The two sides of Rajni's character were sharply etched—when one of his sons was seriously injured in a car accident and was for many weeks in the intensive care ward of Jaslok Hospital, Rajni had a suite of rooms on the ground floor reserved to receive his shoals of visitors. They were served with tea, coffee, Scotch and eats. An intercom kept them informed of the boy's condition. On my last visit to the hospital I was allowed to see the lad. On my way out, an elderly grey-haired but very handsome lady who was sitting on a stool rose up and accosted me: 'Please tell me how the boy is doing,' she said. I told her, adding that she could go in and see for herself. 'I am not allowed to go in,' she replied, without any emotion. This was Susheila Patel, the boy's mother.

GURCHARAN SINGH TOHRA:
BE-TAAJ BADSHAH

The last I saw of Jathedar Gurcharan Singh Tohra was on the TV screen sitting behind *raagis* (hymn singers) in Harimandir, the Golden Temple, It was in the morning. Tohra, as President of the Shiromani Gurdwara Prabandhak Committee, inaugurated the *Kar Seva* (voluntary service) to clean the pool of nectar *(Amritsar)* of the silt that had accumulated in the bottom over the last twenty years. Over two million men and women were expected to take part in it. The hymn the *raagis* were singing was very appropriate: *Satguru kee seva safal hai, jo karey chit laae*—the service of the Lord is fruitful if one puts one's heart and soul in it.

A few hours later he suffered a massive heart attack and was taken to a local hospital. The Prime Minister, Atal Bihari Vajpayee, his deputy, L.K. Advani, Prakash Singh Badal and other Punjabi leaders called on him. Tohra was shifted to Escorts hospital in Delhi in the hope that a heart surgery might save his life. Before it could be done, he gave up the fight and died a few minutes after midnight gave way to the first April. It was not the right time for leaders to go: daily papers are usually put to bed (i.e., ready for printing) and there is little space available on the front page. Besides India was poised for a spectacular victory in the first test match against Pakistan, and Laxmi Pandit had something to say about her age and marital status to win the Miss India world title in the Miss India Beauty contest. Tohra's departure did not get the coverage it deserved.

He dominated Sikh politics for over half-a-century. He could have become the uncrowned king of the Sikhs and have an entire chapter on his life in the history of his community. He did not go very far beyond being the most important *Jathedar* and his name will be found in the footnotes.

Gurcharan Singh Tohra was born in 1924, the son of a small holding farmer in village Tohra (hence the surname) in Patiala district. He was a Tiwana Jat. And like most Jat Sikhs, tall, strapping with an imposing presence. He was a man of modest learning with command over Punjabi and the Holy Scriptures. He spoke Hindustani with a Punjabi accent. He understood English but could not speak it. He made his debut in Sikh politics while he was in his mid-twenties. It was after Partition that the Sikh population of what became Pakistan migrated *en masse* and was scattered all over India, political power passed out of the hands of leaders from west Punjab to those of Malwa and Doaba. Tohra's role in the Partition massacres cast a blemish on his character. He confessed to having taken part in it and killing an innocent Muslim. If he had saved Muslims from the wrath of Sikh and Hindu mobs thirsting for Muslim blood, I would have saluted him as a true leader.

Tohra was elected member of the SGPC in 1960. In 1973, he was elected its president for the first time. And, but for four or five years, he remained its head being re-elected 26 times till the day he died. He could have used the vast resources of money (well over 150 crores a year) and control of innumerable schools, colleges and hospitals managed by the

SGPC; he could well have wiped out illiteracy and educated unemployment from the richest and the most forward-looking agricultural community of India. He did not have the vision to do so. However, it has to be conceded that Tohra was scrupulously honest in money matters, and unlike many politicians, did not add a rupee to his personal wealth nor indulged in nepotism. Also, unlike other politicians he was a puritan: he did not drink, didn't stay in five-star hotels, and did not own a car or a bungalow.

His years as head of the SGPC left another big black mark on his career. He failed to preserve the sanctity of the Golden Temple and allowed Bhindranwale to turn it into an armed fortress, which in turn forced the central government to order the Indian army to enter its sacred precincts. The army not only killed Bhindranwale and hundreds of his armed followers, but also thousands of innocent pilgrims and wrecked the *Akal Takht*. Tohra tamely surrendered to the army and lost much of the respect he had earned. Later an attempt was made on his life.

Tohra was elected to the Rajya Sabha six times and the Lok Sabha once. Not many Indians had so long a run as he in the Parliament. But he rarely took part in the proceedings. His contribution to debates in the Parliament could be written behind a postal stamp.

Tohra had a sneaking sympathy for Khalistan. I recall once confronting him directly on the subject. I told him that over 20 per cent of the Sikh population lived and prospered outside Punjab. Most of them were refugees from Pakistan. Did he want them to be uprooted once again? Didn't he realize that Khalistan would spell disaster for the Khalsa Panth? His reply was a chilling assertion: *'Qauman noon qurbani deynee paundee hai*—communities have to make sacrifices to achieve their goals.'

Tohra was a wily politician who could out-fox anyone who stood in his way. Here was indeed a man who could have become the *Be-Taaj Badshah* of the Panth, but his vision remains limited to launching morchas and going to jail. He did not have the qualities of a visionary statesman who could have led a vibrant and progressive community to greater heights of prosperity and find an honourable place in the annals of history.

The last I saw him was again on TV at the state funeral given to him in his village. There was an enormous crowd of mourners. In the background played the most beautiful dirge: *Saajan maindey rangley jaee suttey jeeraan*—my handsome friend has gone to sleep amongst the dead.

My eyes filled with tears. What great things this man could have accomplished if he had the vision and the will to do so.

DHIREN BHAGAT: GONE AT 30

I was still in my 80s and in robust good health when Dhiren Bhagat wrote a mock obituary on me. I lived on to write Dhiren's obituary after he met his death in a road accident. This is how it went.

A few years ago Dhiren Bhagat wrote my obituary for an Indian journal. Some of it was flattering: my being larger than life and a journalist's father-figure; some not so flattering: my undeserved and self-generated reputation of being a drunkard and a womanizer, whereas I had in fact slept with nothing more animated than a hot water bottle. Most of it was having fun at my expense. Many people, who didn't read beyond the first few lines lamenting my demise, fired off long telegrams and letters of condolence to my 'widow'.

I live to write Dhiren Bhagat's obituary. He is in fact dead. It was an untimely death: he was only 30. A cruel death: he was crushed under a bus while overtaking another. And a singularly tragic one as he was the only child of his parents and a young man with enormous promise as a writer and a journalist.

Dhiren came to see me soon after he returned from Oxford. He was a pretty, effeminate, red-lipped boy in gold-rimmed glasses, dressed, in Khadi kurta-pyjama with a silk shawl draped about his shoulders. He had the cultivated stutter of the English upper class. He had political aspirations and seemed to have acquired the *neta's* (leader's) garb as the first step towards achieving *netahood*. I gathered he was related to my wife whose mother was a Bhagat. I got the impression that he was a phoney.

Then I began to read his articles in *The Spectator*. My opinion of him changed. They were extremely well-researched, witty, and beautifully worded. I became a fan. After reading some of his articles on Punjab, I persuaded him to do a book on the subject and took him to meet President Zail Singh. Thereafter, whenever he happened to be in Delhi, he dropped in to see me. I took him out to dine with friends. Although a teetotaller and a vegetarian, he was great company.

When it came to meeting deadlines, Dhiren proved to be elusive. He always had a plausible excuse: he was short of money and compelled to write for papers to meet his day-to-day expenses. My colleague in Penguin India, David Davidar, agreed with me that we should tie him down with a contract. He was the only author on our list to whom we paid an advance royalty. Then he had another set of excuses: he had become correspondent of *The Observer* (London); he was in love, jilted by his girlfriend and accident-prone; while covering the *Hola Mohalla* at Anandpur, he was knocked down by a cavalry of nihangs and badly bruised. He had to spend several days in hospital. Every time we met he had some good reason for not submitting his manuscript. 'It is not going to be just a journalist's reportage but a work of art,' he would assure me. 'If you want your money back, I'll give you a cheque.' We decided to give him more time. Destiny did not. Penguin India is left poorer by a few thousand rupees; India has lost a man who might well have become one of its most illustrious sons.

PRABHA DUTT: BOSS'S BOSS

It would have been more appropriate if Prabha had written this piece on me rather than I on her. Her pen was still rapier sharp; mine is somewhat blunted with age. She would have used royal-blue ink to write my obituary; I can only use my colourless tears to write hers. For Prabha it was not yet time for the noonday prayer; for me bells peal for evensong. None of these considerations counted with the Divine Reaper. Early one morning when He set out to gather blossoms from the media's flowerbed of lilies, he plucked one still in the prime of her youth and the fairest of them all.

I knew very little of Prabha Dutt before I became her boss. She was the bossy type and instinctively resented anyone lording over her. When she first came to see me in my office she made it quite clear that she wasn't the kind of person who took orders from anyone; she knew her job better than I and if I minded my business, she would mind hers. She regarded me with her large, grey eyes as an insect-collector would examine the latest beetle in his collection and put me several questions framed to find out what kind of editor I would make. I was somewhat overawed by her presence and the *viva voce* test she put me through. It took me several months to break through her impersonal, no-nonsense attitude towards me and persuade her to accept the hand of friendship I extended to her.

The breakthrough was dramatic. Prabha was as much married to *The Hindustan Times* as she was to her husband and as involved with the paper as she was with her two daughters. And extremely touchy about both. It was after one of her many outbursts against a colleague who got away with very little work that she dissolved into tears of rage. I was able to take the liberty of putting a paternal arm round her shoulders. She shrugged it off but thereafter did me the honour of treating me as her father-in-office to whom she could turn in moments of crisis.

In Prabha's scheme of values work took precedence over everything else. This gave her enormous courage to speak her mind without bothering whom she was speaking to and writing without concern of consequences that might follow. In my presence she told K.K. Birla to his face what was wrong with *The Hindustan Times*. She busted financial and social rackets (she had a lady-like disdain for sex scandals) and was often threatened with violence. The one and only time she quarrelled with me was when I tried to withhold her story on S.L. Khurana who had been Executive President of *The Hindustan Times* and was then Lieutenant Governor of Delhi. I have little doubt that if she had found out something about my evading taxes, smuggling contraband or involvement in some shady deal, despite her affection for me, she would not have spared me.

Prabha was a very conservative, straight-laced person passionately devoted to her family, friends, servants and their families. She not only spent every moment she could spare from work teaching her and her servants' children but eagerly took on the problems of her friends on her own shoulders. She

was as fierce in her loyalties towards people she befriended as
she could be aggressively unfriendly and outspokenly offensive
to their detractors. These characteristics gave her the image of
one who was hard as nail and quick of temper. Those who
knew her better realized how soft she really was: every
outburst of temper was followed by a cascade of tears. She was
like the cactus, prickly on the outside, sugar-sweet within.

Had Prabha a premonition that she had a short time to go?
I am not sure. She certainly crammed in as much activity for
her two daughters as any mother would who felt she may soon
be parted from them. On the other hand, a day before her
haemorrhage she went to see a relative in hospital and told him
very cheerfully how lucky he was to be lying comfortably in
bed without having to bother about going to office. Little did
she then know that within a few hours she would be in the
same hospital fighting a losing battle for her own life. Her
closest friend, Usha Rai, told me that the evening before she
died, as Usha was rubbing her hands, Prabha asked her in a
feeble voice: 'Are you reading the lines on my palm? Tell me
will I leave this hospital alive?'

In all my years in journalism I have yet to meet as gutsy a
girl with integrity that brooked no compromise, daring that
verged on foolhardiness, total dedication to her work with
contempt for the *kaamchor* (shirker), than Prabha Dutt. I am
glad to see that her daughter Barkha Dutt of NDTV has not
only inherited her mother's looks but also her fearlessness and
dedication to her work.

HARDAYAL: A TRIBUTE TO THE GREAT REVOLUTIONARY

While I was still at school, the one name that was on all lips as the paradigm of the ultimate in scholarship was that of Hardayal. His name was always prefixed by two words—the great: he was the great Hardayal. Stories of his greatness as a student multiplied. He had a phenomenal memory: he had to read a book once and he could reproduce its contents word for word; he was not only a topper in every subject, but he also broke previous records with wide margins in every exam he took. Though this was not absolutely correct because at times he was beaten by other examinees to the second place, but people refused to believe it. What made his reputation impregnable was the fact that he was also a revolutionary who spurned government patronage, directed the Ghadar Movement in its early years in the US and Canada, became the principal adviser of the German Government's attempt to foment a revolt against the British Raj during World War I. Then like his equally distinguished contemporary, Veer Savarkar, he took a complete somersault, apologized for his past errors and pledged loyalty to them. One may well ask, if Veer Savarkar's portrait can be hung in our Parliament, why not Hardayal's?

What was the truth about Hardayal's alleged greatness? At long last we have a biography written by his granddaughter and her husband which sifts fact from fiction: *Hardayal: The Great Revolutionary* by E. Jaiwant & Shubh Paul (Roli Books).

Hardayal was born in Delhi on 4 October 1884, the sixth of seven children of Bhoti and Gauri Dayal Mathur, Reader of the District Court. He went to Cambridge Mission School and graduated from St. Stephen's College. He won a stipend and joined Government College, Lahore. He took his MA in English language and literature and another MA in history, breaking the university record for the highest marks. He won a scholarship to St. John's College, Oxford. While in India, he had been impressed by Christian missionaries' selfless dedication, the Arya and Brahmo Samaj's attempts to purify Hinduism of meaningless rituals and superstition. He admired Lala Lajpat Rai and befriended Bhai Parmanand.

Hardayal joined Oxford University in 1905. He was 21 and married. He could have easily walked into any government job but had by now been infected by the bug of patriotism. 'To hell with the ICS,' he said and refused to take the examination. He got to know Dadabhai Naoroji and Shyamaji Krishna Verma and decided to throw his lot in the freedom struggle. He returned the stipend money to the government and quit Oxford.

He was somewhat of an ascetic. He never drank nor smoked. He turned vegetarian, shed European clothes and took to wearing kurta and dhoti. He always slept on the floor. He studied different religions and regarded Buddha as his role model. He discussed the possibility of starting a new religion with Bhai Parmanand, who dissuaded him from doing so, saying, 'My own view is that all religions are a kind of fraud on mankind. You will be merely adding one more fraud.'

Hardayal made a meagre living by delivering lectures on Indian philosophy and writing articles. He edited Madam Cama's *Bande Matram* and *Talwar*. In 1911, he went to

America to study Buddhism at Harvard. Stanford University invited him to teach Indian philosophy. His radical views—he advocated free love—ended his tenure at Stanford. He had also taken up with a Swiss girl, Fried Hauswirth, which scandalized his American and Indian admirers. While still at Stanford, Hardayal made contacts with Indian workers in the West Coast and went across to help them organize the Ghadar Party. When they got news of the attempt to kill Viceroy Hardinge on 23 December 1912, in Delhi, Hardayal was amongst other Indians at Berkeley to celebrate the occasion, doing *bhangra* and singing *Bande Matram*.

The Ghadar Party was formed on 1 November 1913, with Hardayal as its guiding spirit. He was arrested by the US police and on release decided to go to Switzerland to rejoin Fried Hauswirth. In turn she came to the US to formalize her divorce and instead of joining Hardayal, married another Indian, Sarangdhar Das.

World War I broke out on 4 August 1914. Hardayal spent the early years of the war in Germany and Turkey, planning an invasion of India by a liberation force. He was naive enough to believe that the Germans were eager to see India a free country. It took him a long time to see through the subterfuge and he turned a bitter critic of Germans and Turks. Of the latter, he opined: 'Turks have no brains... as a nation they are utterly unfit to assume the leadership of the Muslim world.' Of the Germans, who had financed his ventures, he wrote that they were 'without character... avaricious. They work hard and are patriotic but that is perhaps their only virtue.' He became an ardent admirer of the British as a 'truthful people... who had a moral and historical mission in India'. The British government had his pronouncements translated into Hindi and distributed free in India.

Hardayal had nowhere to go except to a neutral country. He chose Sweden. He had taken up with a Swedish woman,

Agda Erikson, and with some difficulty managed to get a Swedish visa. He spent many years in Sweden, learnt to speak Swedish and 13 other languages. He lived with Agda, who described herself as Mrs. Hardayal. He wrote several books of which *Hints on Self Culture* is the best known and sells to this day. He was allowed to return to England and was finally granted amnesty by the British with permission to go back to India. He was never able to do so. While on a lecture tour of the US, he died in his sleep in Philadelphia on 4 March 1939. He was only 54.

A heart-broken Agda Erikson took his ashes back to her native Sweden. That was all the great Hardayal left for her. His worldly wealth, for what it was worth, he left for his wife and her daughter Shanti who he never saw.

RGK: PARADIGM OF SELF-EFFACEMENT

There are people who do what they think is their duty (*karma*) to the best of their ability without caring whether or not they get recognition or monetary compensation for it: they are true examples of the exhortation in the *Bhagavadgita*: *Karmanyev adhikarstey ma phaleshu kadahchana* (Perform your duty without consideration of the fruits thereof). One such person who came into my life for nine long years was RGK. He was on the staff of *The Illustrated Weekly of India* when I took over as editor. He stayed on after I was sacked. The management ignored my recommendation that he take over from me. Without the slightest concern, he continued to do the job under a succession of editors—Kamath, Khanna, Pritish Nandy—till he retired. He died a couple of weeks ago, unhonoured and unsung.

Despite being in daily contact with him for almost a decade when he was my number two, I knew very little about him besides that the 'G' in his initials RGK stood for Gopal, the name with which we called him. He wrote more for *The Weekly* than any other member of the staff, but did not want any credit or byline besides his initials. He was one man we

relied on to write on different aspects of Hinduism because he
knew all the sacred texts in their Sanskrit originals.

All the time he worked for the journal he sat on a corner
table of the large hall which also accommodated the staff of
Dharmyug, Femina and *Filmfare*. Behind him were urinals and
toilets. Newcomers and visitors who wanted to use the facility
often interrupted RGK in his work to ask 'Where is the loo?'
He put a placard on his table reading 'Toilets straight ahead.'
He did not have a great sense of humour. I never heard him
laugh and rarely saw a smile on his face.

We knew he was South Indian but not sure whether he
was from Andhra, Karnataka, Tamil Nadu or Kerala. Once
Bikram Vohra asked RGK, 'Are you Malayalu?' RGK replied,
'How would you like if I asked you "Are you Punjaboo?" ' And
that was that.

Not many people from the *Times of India* group of
newspapers and journals knew of RGK's existence. He could
not care less if no one in the world knew about him. Grey's
verse applied to him:

Full many a gem of purest ray serene
Dark, unfathomed caves of the ocean bear;
Full many a flower is born to blush unseen
And waste its sweetness in the desert air.

REMEMBERING MULK, THE PIONEER

Way back in the 1940s a few friends with literary ambitions formed a circle which met once a week to read poems and stories we had written. It was a mutual admiration society where glasses of whisky were refilled at the end of each recitation. We heard of Indian writers Mulk Raj Anand and R.K. Narayan making good in England with publication of their novels. Eagerly we laid our hands on their books and discussed them in our meetings. We were a conceited lot and were generally agreed that if Mulk Raj and Narayan could find publishers abroad, so could we. When Mulk visited Punjab after making a name for himself in England, he was acclaimed as a pioneer of Indo-Anglian writing. He agreed to come to one of our meetings. He expected to be lionized; he was visibly put off with the cool reception he got. 'You chaps don't know what it takes to write a novel,' he snapped, 'talk to me after you have had one accepted by a publisher.' He had every right to snub us.

My view of Mulk and Narayan has not changed over the years. Both were indeed pioneers of Indo-Anglian fiction in their own way, prolific in their output but mediocre craftsmen. Mulk's novels were propaganda stuff with a sheen of fiction:

Untouchable, Coolie, Two Leaves and a Bud. They were designed to rouse the conscience of readers to the indignities inflicted by the well-to-do on the poor and make Britishers feel guilty about their racist colonialism. He was duly lauded by British Liberals and Leftists. Narayan was content to remain a storyteller, combining simple themes about people living at a leisurely pace in an imaginary small town—Malgudi. He was more widely acclaimed than Mulk, particularly in South India. But both had one thing in common—they were both pioneers.

Mulk was born in Peshawar (12 December 1905) but spent his formative years in school and college in Amritsar. He often described himself as an *Umbersaria*. He was of short stature with a mop of curly hair and a pouting lower lip. He was never at a loss for words and could hold forth by the hour and often waffling *thuth, thuth* when he was worked up. Even when addressing a meeting where every speaker was given five to ten minutes to speak, Mulk would go on rambling for half-an-hour, taking no notice of the bell to tell him his time was over, nor a tap on his shoulder. He often dwelt at length on how his father often beat his mother, and what effect it had on him as a child. He never forgave his father and was diagnosed by no lesser a psychoanalyst than Dr Sigmund Freud as suffering from acute mother-fixation.

Mulk was very proud of being an Indian, of India's great legacy of art, sculpture, painting, its style of architecture (havelis), its way of living and etiquette. Once at a ghazal concert in London, he sat in the first row and applauded at the end of every couplet and was acknowledged by a polite *salaam*. No one else in the audience knew it was the polite thing to do. An English friend I had taken with me asked me in a whisper, 'Who is that little fellow barking "Wow! Wow!" while the fellow is singing?' I told him who Mulk was and that he was not barking but saying '*Wah! Wah!*, Wonderful! Wonderful!', which was the done thing.

Although Mulk spent some time with Gandhiji in his ashram, he was much closer to the Communist Party in his politics. He was closely affiliated to the Progressive Writers Association and the People's Theatre Group. This made him an anathema to right wingers. Once he was foolish enough to become an easy target for them. He was invited by *Evergreen Review* of New York to write a long article on the erotic in Indian Art. A week after the article appeared profusely illustrated with pictures of sculptures from Khajuraho and paintings from *Kamasutra*, the magazine received a legal notice from Prof. Campbell of Sarah Lawrence College of New York alleging the article had been lifted from his translation from German on the same subject. Poor Mulk was asked to elucidate. He took great pains trying to exonerate himself. This was good enough for Communist-baiter Dosu Karaka, editor of *Current* to splash the news on the front page of his weekly tabloid with the banner headline 'Commie writer caught plagiarizing.' It took many months for Mulk to be able to appear in public.

I visited Mulk a couple of times in his ground floor flat on Cuffe Parade in Mumbai. He had a specially designed high chair with a slab in front to place his papers to write. It looked very much like a baby's chair put alongside a dining table. Mulk sat on it resting his feet on the rung below and scribbled away by the hour.

Though no Casanova, women of different nationalities were drawn to him like moths to a flame. He was a celebrity and they enjoyed being seen with him. He married more than twice and had several lady friends. His one child through an English wife co-authored a most readable biography of Maharaja Dalip Singh.

Mulk's lasting legacy is *Marg*, a magazine devoted to the arts financed by the Tatas. It had, and has, a limited circulation but is unique being the only one on the subject and of high quality. He received many awards including one from Sahitya Akademi and a Padma Bhushan. His word counted a great deal in official circles, particularly amongst senior Babus who knew no more than the titles of his books, but were awed by his reputation. He was able to persuade them to make grants for writers' homes in Delhi and Lonavala. Usually he was the sole occupant of these homes.

What I have written may not sound like a tribute to a celebrated author. For this I crave pardon from Mulk's millions of admirers. But when I heard of his death in Pune on 28 September 2004 at the age of 99, I was overcome with grief. I may not have held him in great esteem as a writer, but I recall him with great affection.

THE ONE AND ONLY NIRAD BABU

'There is nothing more dreadful to an author than neglect, compared with which reproach, hatred and opposition are names of happiness.' These words of Dr Johnson were inscribed by Nirad Chaudhuri on my copy of his book, *A Passage to England*. These words hold the key to Nirad Babu's past life and present personality. They explain the years of neglect of one who must have at all times been a most remarkable man; his attempt to attract attention by cocking a snook at people who had neglected him; and the 'reproach, hatred and opposition' that he succeeded in arousing as a result of his rudeness.

Nirad Babu had been writing in Bengali for many years. But it was not until the publication of his first book in English, *The Autobiography of an Unknown Indian*, that he really aroused the interest of the class to which he belonged and which, because of the years of indifference to him, he had come heartily to loathe—the Anglicized upper-middle class of India. He did this with calculated contempt. He knew that the wogs were more English than Indian, but were fond of proclaiming their patriotism at the expense of the British. That having lost their own traditions and not having fully imbibed those of England, they were a breed with pretensions to intellectualism that seldom went beyond reading the blurbs and reviews of books.

He therefore decided to dedicate the work 'To the British Empire...' The wogs took the bait, and having only read the dedication, sent up a howl of protest. Many people who would not have otherwise read the autobiography, discovered to their surprise that there was nothing anti-Indian in its pages. On the contrary, it was the most beautiful picture of eastern Bengal that anyone had ever painted.

And at long last, India had produced a writer who did not cash in on naive Indianisms but could write the English language as it should be written—and as few, if any, living Englishmen could write.

Nobody could afford to ignore Nirad Chaudhuri any more. He and his wife Amiya became the most sought-after couple in Delhi's upper-class circles. Anecdotes of his vast fund of knowledge were favourite topics at dinner parties.

The first story I heard of the Chaudhuri family was of a cocktail party hosted by the late Director-General of All India Radio, Colonel Lakshmanan. Nirad Babu had brought his wife, and sons (in shorts and full boots) to the function, After the introductions, the host asked what Nirad Babu would like to drink, and mentioned that he had some excellent sherry.

'What kind of sherry?' asked the chief guest. Colonel Lakshmanan had, like most people, heard of only two kinds. 'Both kinds,' he replied. 'Do you like dry or sweet?' This wasn't good enough for Nirad Babu, so he asked one of his sons to taste it and tell him. The thirteen-year-old lad took a sip, rolled it about his tongue, and after a thoughtful pause replied, 'Must be an Oloroso 1947.'

Nirad Babu could talk about any subject under the sun. There was not a bird, tree, butterfly or insect whose name he did not know in Latin, Sanskrit, Hindi and Bengali. Long before he left for London, he not only knew where the important monuments and museums were, but also the location of many famous restaurants. I heard him contradict a lady who had lived six years in Rome about the name of a street leading off from the Colosseum—and prove his contention. I've heard him discuss stars with astronomers, recite lines from an obscure fifteenth century French literary text and advise a wine dealer on the best vintages from Burgundy. At a small function in honour of Laxness, the Icelandic winner of the Nobel Prize for literature, I heard Nirad Babu lecture him on Icelandic literature.

Nirad Babu was a small, frail man, little over five feet. He led a double life. At home he dressed in *dhoti-kurta* and sat on the floor to do his reading and writing. When leaving for work, he wore the European dress: coat, tie, trousers and a monstrous khaki sola topi. As soon as he stepped out, street urchins would chant 'Johnnie Walker, left, right, left, right.'

Nirad Babu was not a modest man; he had great reason to be immodest. No Indian, living or dead, wrote the English language as well as he did. He was also a very angry man. When he was dismissed from service by a singularly half-baked I&B minister, Dr B.V. Keskar, he exploded with wrath. Years later, the Government of India wanted him to do a definitive booklet on the plight of the Hindu minority in East Pakistan and offered him a blank cheque for his services. Nirad Babu, who was in dire financial straits, turned it down with contempt. 'The Government may have lifted its ban on Nirad Chaudhuri, but Nirad Chaudhuri has not lifted his ban on the Government of India,' he said to me when I conveyed Finance Minister T.T. Krishnamachari's proposal to him.

Nirad Babu's second book, *A Passage to England*, received the most glorious reviews in the English press. Three editions were rapidly sold out and it had the distinction of becoming the first book by an Indian author to have become a bestseller in England. The bay windows of London's famous bookshop, Foyles, were decorated with large-sized photographs of Nirad Babu. Some Indian critics were, as in the past, extremely hostile. Nirad Babu's reaction followed the same pattern. At first he tried nor to be bothered by people 'who didn't know better', then burst out with invectives against the 'yapping curs'. I asked him how he reconciled himself to these two attitudes. After a pause he replied, 'When people say nasty things about my books without really understanding what I have written, I feel like a father who sees a drunkard make an obscene pass at his daughter. I want to chastise him.' Then, with a typically Bengali gesture demonstrating the form of chastisement, 'I want to give them a shoe-beating with my *chappal*.'

A few years ago Nirad Babu wrote an article for a prestigious London weekly in which he mentioned how hard he was finding life in Oxford, living on his royalties from books. I published extracts from it in my column. K.K. Birla wrote to me to tell Nirad Babu that he would be happy to give him a stipend for life for any amount in any currency he wanted. I forwarded Birla's letter to Nirad Babu. He wrote back asking me to thank Birla for his generous offer, but refused to accept it.

It is a pity that he accepted a CBE (Commander of the British Empire) from the British Government. He deserved a peerage, because he was in fact, a peerless man of intellect and letters.

BALWANT GARGI: THE NAKED TRIANGLE FETCHED HIM MORE FOES THAN FRIENDS

A sixty-year-old friendship ended on 22 April 2003. Balwant Gargi who I had befriended in my Lahore days died in Mumbai. His body was flown to Delhi to be cremated. Amongst the Punjabi litterateurs who were present was former Prime Minister I.K. Gujral. The film world was represented by Anupam Kher. Unfortunately, only Punjabi papers carried tributes to the versatile genius because besides two or three books, he wrote mostly in Gurmukhi script.

Balwant was a *bania* from Bathinda. He moved to Lahore which was once the centre of Punjabi writing. He made his name as a playwright, director and a writer of satires: his profiles of well-known writers were full of acid wit. After Partition he moved to Delhi where he acquired a tiny, one-room ground floor apartment with a small courtyard and a kitchen on one side, a lavatory on the other. He entertained friends in his bed-cum-sitting-cum-dining room.

The room had no furniture and all his guests had to sit or sprawl on the floor while drinking or eating. Only a few people were privileged enough to be invited to his home. Though a podgy, flabby *bania,* forever washing his hands with invisible soap, he had an eye for beautiful women with a marked preference for *sardarnis* (female Sikhs). I often chided him, 'You have this *chaska* (taste) for Sikh women; I suspect because only Sikh women can read you in Gurmukhi script.'

I persuaded him to try his hand in English to widen his circle of admirers. He did. His work on Indian theatre was well received. He was invited by Washington State University (Seattle) to teach courses in drama. For the first time he came into some money. He returned with a large car and a pretty American wife, Jeannie. They moved to Chandigarh where he was appointed Professor of Dramatics. Everyone who met Jeannie fell in love with her. But she remained loyal to her husband. Her only shortcoming was her enormous appetite for food—at one sitting she could eat food enough for three people—and her refusal to learn Punjabi. Though she gave Balwant two lovely children, a boy and a girl, she refused to learn Punjabi and was unable to give him the praise he hankered after. So he turned to others, including an attractive divorcee who was one of his students. Needless to say, she was a *sardarni* and had been his pre-marriage mistress. Jeannie divorced him, married another Indian and returned to the States, taking her daughter with her. Balwant was left with his son and a wayward mistress. When she ditched him for another man, he took revenge by writing an autobiographical novel in English, *The Naked Triangle*. It was a bad novel written in bitterness. Instead of gaining more admirers, he lost some he had.

I saw a lot of Balwant Gargi. He was a most engaging conversationalist. Through him, I met actress Parveen Babi when she was queen of Bollywood. Uma Vasudev was also a regular fixture at his dinner parties.

Balwant Gargi sensed his end coming four years before it came. He rang me up from Patiala to thank me for all I had done for him. It was uncalled for because I had done little besides lending him money when he was hard up (he always returned it) and advising him to write in English. I ticked him off: 'What's the matter with you?' and 'You owe me nothing; we are old friends.'

He knew he was stricken with Alzheimer's disease and would soon lose his memory. He spent his last years with his actor son in Mumbai, being looked after by a faithful servant and a lady friend, a *sardarni*.

R.K. NARAYAN: MALGUDI NO MORE

A week before he died at 95, news of his precarious health began appearing in all national dailies. I got calls from some, including the BBC and other television channels to be ready with a tribute—in case. It showed the worldwide concern and regard people had for R.K. Narayan. On Sunday, 13 May 2001 at 5 a.m. my telephone rang. It was from the BBC in London. Narayan had died two hours earlier and would I say something about him. I did, in Hindi, for the Hindi service and in English for the home services.

Narayan deserved the adulation heaped on him. He was the leader of the quartet comprising Raja Rao, Mulk Raj Anand and Govind Desani which proved to the English-speaking world that Indians could handle their language as well as writers born to it. Narayan was luckier than his contemporaries in finding an enthusiastic patron in Graham Greene who launched his writing career, persuading publishers to offer him lucrative contracts. He was the first to spot Narayan's deceptively simple prose shorn of purple passages, completely free of sex or violence which most writers exploit to hold the readers' interest. Narayan put his imaginary one-horse town

Malgudi on the world map. His slow-moving, languid plots and characters were replicas of life and people of southern India. He found ardent admirers in N. Ram and his English wife, Susan, who jointly wrote his well-researched voluminous biography and opened up columns of *The Hindu* to him, which made Narayan the most widely read Indo-Anglian writer in the South. In the North, grudging acceptance of his craftsmanship came much later. Frank Moraes, the most celebrated editor of recent times, found Narayan's novels 'tedious reading'.

I first met Narayan when he was living in the suburbs of Mysore. He worked in the mornings and came into the town late in the afternoon. I accompanied him on his walks through the bazaar. He walked very slowly and stopped every few yards to complete what he was saying. He stopped at many shops to exchange *namaskaras* with shopkeepers, introduced me to them and conversed in Kannada or Tamil, neither of which I understood. We resumed our leisurely stroll.

When he was in Delhi, he dropped by as often as he could to have a cup of coffee and a chat with me. We also met at writers' conferences in England and America. The one meeting which remains etched in my mind is a week we spent together in Hawaii. Having said our pieces, we spent our evenings together. He was not great company. I found his habit of suddenly stopping after every few steps to finish what he was saying somewhat frustrating. Finding a good place to have an evening meal also posed a problem. He was a strict teetotaller and vegetarian; I was neither. He would go to a grocery store and buy a carton of plain yogurt (*dahi*). Then we would go from one eatery to another to find out if they had what Narayan needed. 'Do you have plain boiled rice?' The answer was usually in the negative. When we found one, Narayan would get his plateful of boiled rice and empty the carton of yogurt on it. He would have liked to use his fingers to eat it but condescended to use his spoon.

One evening, I decided to shake him off and either find a more sociable companion or go out alone. When he came to pick me up, I told him that I wanted to go to see a blue movie which he may not like. 'I'll come along, I don't mind,' he assured me. We went to a sleazy part of Honolulu which had several cinema houses showing blue movies. We chose one, bought our tickets and went in. It was showing sex in the most vulgar forms. I thought Narayan would walk out, or throw up. He sat placidly without making any comment. It was I who said 'Let's go.' He turned kindly to me and asked, 'You've had enough?'

Narayan's gentle, shy, laid-back manners gave the impression that he was a very humble, modest man. Humble he was, but not modest. Once when All India Radio invited writers to give talks on literature and offered fees much higher than the usual, all writers accepted its offer. Only Narayan made one condition that he should get at least Re 1 more than the others. In his travelogue, *My Dateless Diary* he writes about a lunch given in his honour. During the course of the conversation, one of the guests remarked that he thought R.K. Narayan was one of the three greatest novelists of the times and named the other two. Another guest disagreed about the other two but included Narayan's name in his list of three greats.

I wrote about this in one of my columns. Narayan never spoke to me again.

Now that he is gone, I miss his presence as much as millions of his admirers. A fitting tribute to him would be to name some town in Karnataka or Tamil Nadu after the locale of his novels and short stories—Malgudi.

ALI SARDAR JAFRI:
THE POETRY OF BURNING

The day Ali Sardar Jafri died in Bombay on 1 August 2000, at 8.30 a.m., I made it a point to watch Pakistan Television to find out what it had to say about him. He was not only in the front-rank of Urdu poets of recent times but also the spearhead of the movement for a rapprochement with Pakistan. Pak TV made a passing reference to Jafri's death as a poet who wrote of the need for love and understanding between people. I was disappointed. So was I with the coverage given by the Indian media, both the print and the electronic. There was a lot more to Jafri than the hastily written obituaries and collages put together to meet deadlines.

I had known Ali Sardar and his beautiful wife Sultana for over 30 years. During my years in Bombay we met each other almost every other week. Despite his commitment to Communism, he liked the good things of life: good Scotch, good food and comfortable living. He lived in a pokey little three-room flat off Peddar Road. Apart from his wife and three children who often stayed with him, he had two widowed sisters in the same apartment. There was not much room to move about. Many of his books were stacked under his bed on which he read, wrote

and slept. I would arrive armed with a bottle of Scotch. He
would send for soda and biryani from a restaurant, Allah Beli,
facing his apartment. I sought his company because he was
about the most erudite of Indian writers I had met.

Ali Sardar also had a phenomenal memory. If I quoted one
line of any Urdu poet, he would come out with the rest of the
poem. And explain every word by referring to Persian poets—
from Rumi and Hafiz to Ghalib and Allama Iqbal. When I set
about translating Iqbal's *Shikwa* and *Jawab-e-Shikwa*, I went all
the way to Bombay to seek his assistance. For two days Ali
Sardar and Sultana came to my hotel in the morning; we
worked till lunchtime when Rafiq Zakaria and his wife Fatma
joined us to find out how it was going. After they left, we
resumed our labours till it was time for our sundowners.

I often needled Ali Sardar about his Communism. He had
been a cardholder and had been expelled from the Aligarh
Muslim University (which later gave him an honorary
doctorate) and spent 18 months in jail during the British Raj
and again after Independence under Morarji Desai. Although
he had ceased to be a cardholder, he stoutly defended Marxist
ideology. What was beyond my comprehension was that
despite professing atheism, during the month of Moharrum he
often wore black and attended Shia majlises and abstained
from alcohol. During a TV interview with me, when he
expected to be questioned about Urdu poetry, I confronted
him with his contradictory beliefs in both Islam and Marxism.
He was visibly upset and fumbled for words. He took it out on
me after the interview was over. He called me everything
under the sun short of calling me a bastard. I am sure if he had
not been so obsessed with Communism and social problems,
he would have made a greater poet.

I saw him often when he came to Delhi to record Kamna
Prasad's series, *Kahkashaan* (Milky Way), on contemporary
Urdu poets. And later to participate in the *Jashn-e-Bahaar*

mushairas organized by Kamna to bring Pakistani and Urdu poets together on one stage every year. He presided over the last one a few months before he died.

He had an imposing presence: he was a lean, tall man with a mop of untidy, tousled grey hair, sparkling dark eyes and an ever-smiling face. His voice held his audience spellbound. His message to Pakistan at a time when Indo-Pak relations were at their worst was one of peace:

Tum aao gulshan-e-Lahore se chaman bardosh,
Hum aayen subh-e-Banaras ki roshnee le kar
Himalay ki havaaon ki taazgee le kar
Aur iske baad yeh poochein ki kaun dushman hai?

(You come from the garden of Lahore laden with flowers,
We will come bearing the light of a Benaras morning
With fresh breezes from Himalayan heights
And then, together we can ask, who is the enemy?)

Ali Sardar was an incorrigible optimist. Inspired by Rumi's line, *Hum cho sabza baarha roeeda aym* (like the green of the earth we never stop growing), he summed up his life story (*Mera Safar*) in a few memorable lines:

I am a fleeting moment
In the magic house of days and nights;
I am a restless drop travelling eternally
From the flask of the past to the goblet of the future.
I sleep and wake, awaken to sleep again
I am the ancient play on the stage of time
I die only to become immortal.

Ali Sardar, who was born into a zamindar family in Balrampur (Uttar Pradesh) on 29 November 1913, won numerous awards for his poems, short stories, plays and articles. They included the Iqbal Sanmaan, Soviet Land Nehru Award, Jnaneshwar award and the Jnanpeeth award. More than all those it was the warm-hearted applause he won wherever he went, the respect and affection he received from people he knew that sustained him during his difficult days. He returned the love he got in full measure. In a collection of his poems he gave to Kamna's four-year-old daughter Jia, he wrote the word *pyaar* in Urdu five times on each line down 20 lines. That was his parting message to the world.

FAIZ AHMED FAIZ:
MARXIST, LOVER AND POET

There is a custom amongst Shia Muslims of northern India of tying a charm known as *imam zamin* on the arm of a person about to undertake a long journey. It consists of wrapping a silver coin or currency note in a handkerchief and knotting it around the arm of the traveller with a few words of prayer for his safety. My friend Mahmud Hashmi, Producer in the Urdu service of All India Radio, is of the opinion that this Muslim counterpart of Christopher, the patron saint of travellers, is the poet Imam Zamin buried on the eastern side of Alai Durwaza of the Qutab Minar complex and is therefore post-17th century AD. The custom is no longer confined to Shias and is prevalent amongst Sunni Memons of Maharashtra. Variations of the custom also exist amongst Punjabi Hindus and Sikhs in the form of *sir vaarna* where an elder waves a sum of money over the head of the departing person and gives it to him to spend on his journey. My grandmother, whose bounty seldom exceeded one rupee, used to chant a doggerel which went as follows:

Radd balaaeen
Door balaaeen
Tor taaeen
Rakhey saaeen.

A rough translation would be:

Fie evil spirits.
Go away evil spirits.
To the end of your destination,
May the Lord be your protector.

This time when I went abroad (Japan, Korea and Hong Kong) no one performed *sir vaarna* nor tied an *imam zamin* on my arm. Nevertheless, I came to no harm but what I inflicted on my own person through excessive intake of food and liquor. I had very little to do, too many receptions to attend and a wife keeping her hawk eyes on me to prevent mine from straying. The only pastime left to me was to make a pig of myself on Chinese and Korean delicacies. I dread going on the weighing machine till after I have shed some of the fat I have accumulated.

I confess it was the first time that I did not mind being in the dark about what was happening in my country. It was only on my return that I learnt that Yashwantraoji had died. I had great respect and affection for him as a person but very little of either for him as a politician. Many of my ambitious politician friends had been denied party tickets to fight the forthcoming elections. I felt sorry for some of them. But most of all I was distressed to discover that on the 20th of November when I was having a wonderful time in Tokyo my friend Faiz Ahmed Faiz was dying in Lahore.

I will not say very much about Y.B. Chavan because much had already been written on him. Instead I will write about

Faiz because there could not be many Indians who knew him
as well as I. He was two years my senior at college (and exactly
five years older to the day than my wife, having the same
birthday). He was studying for Masters' degrees in English and
Arabic. Though a student, he had been admitted to the
charmed circle of Lahore's Aesthetes Club comprising
Professor A.S. Bokhari (Patras), Imtiaz Ali Taj, Taseer and Sufi
Tabassum. That was due to his reputation as an up-and-
coming poet. He had been composing poetry ever since he was
sixteen and at his very first public appearance at a mushaira in
Murray College, Sialkot, from where he had taken a bachelor's
degree, he had made his mark with a couplet:

Lab bund hain saaqi, meree aankhon ko pilaa
Voh jaam jo minnatkash-e-sehba nahin hota.

(My lips are sealed Saqi, let these eyes of mine take a sip
Without my begging for more wine.)

A few years later when I returned from England and made my
home in Lahore, we resumed our acquaintance. Following
instructions of the Communist Party of India, Faiz had joined
the British army and wore an officer's uniform. It was about
this time that Alys, whose elder sister was married to Taseer,
came to India to marry Harkirat Singh (later a general) to
whom she had been engaged while he was a cadet at
Sandhurst. By then Harkirat had been married off to a Sikh
girl. Alys was heartbroken. On the rebound she married Faiz
and bore him two daughters: Saleema and Muneeza.

Faiz was no lady-killer. He was of short stature with a dark-
brown complexion which looked as if it had been massaged
with oil. He was a man of few words, soft-spoken and
impassive. It was not his conversation but his poetry that made
him the centre of attraction at every party. Besides his genius

he was remarkably free of any kind of prejudice, racial or religious. Many of his closest friends were Hindus and Sikhs. He was a humanist in the best sense of the word. There were many contradictions in his character. In his writings he championed the cause of the poor and the downtrodden, his style of living was that of an aristocrat: his daily consumption of premium brand of Scotch and imported cigarettes would have fed a worker's family for a month. However, he readily deprived himself of these luxuries to live on rations of dry bread and water given to him when he was in prison.

The Partition of India left deep wounds on Faiz's mind. Although he decided to stay on in the country where he was born, he refused to accept the division between the people and remained to the end of his days Pakistani, Indian and Bangladeshi. He had as little patience with national divisions as he had for the racial or the religious. He was a Communist but more at ease amongst Capitalists, a man who denied God and was yet most god-fearing.

No sooner Pakistan was founded than Faiz found himself deep in trouble. He had a stint as editor of the *Pakistan Times* till he, along with Sajjad Zaheer and some army officers, was arrested and charged with treason. It was during his trial in the Rawalpindi conspiracy case that the chief prosecutor Habibullah, who represented the government in court by day, would visit Faiz in prison in the evening to chant Faiz's compositions to him. Faiz received a sentence of seven years' imprisonment. While serving his sentence in Hyderabad (Sind) jail he was taken seriously ill and removed to a Karachi hospital for treatment. The lady superintendent of the hospital risked her job, her reputation and her neck to whisk Faiz away to her home for a night to feed him and minister to his needs in exchange of listening to him recite his own poetry. The years in jail brought the best out of him as a poet. Being in prison, he once said, was like falling in love again:

Bujha je rauzan-e-zindaan to dil yeh samjha hai
Ke teyree maang sitaron say bhar gaee hogee,
Chamak uthey hain silasil, to ham nay jaanan hai
Kay a sahar teyrey rukh par bikhar gaee hogee.

(When light in my prison window fades and comes the night I
think of your dark tresses and stars twinkling in the parting.
When chains that bind me sparkle in the light
I see your face lit up with the light of the morning.)

A change of government brought Faiz out of jail. Kingsley
Martin, Editor of the *New Statesman and Nation* who visited
him before coming to Delhi to stay with me, told me that for
him the most memorable event in Pakistan was going with Faiz
to Heera Mandi, the prostitutes' quarter, where girls in the
brothel entertained them with Faiz's *ghazals* and instead of
asking for money loaded him with gifts and compliments. Faiz
was no whoremonger, on the contrary he was a puritan who
accorded prostitutes the same respect he did to his sisters.
Life, he wrote, is like a beggar's cloak full of patches of pain
sewn on it.

Faiz was as much in and out of prison as he was in and out
of Pakistan. It was my friend, the late Manzur Qadir, who as
Foreign Minister persuaded President Ayub Khan that the best
way of dealing with a man like Faiz was to honour him and give
him a big job. He was made President of the National Council
of Arts and provided with a spacious bungalow. Thereafter, it
was more Scotch than sonnets of love. When I was invited to
Islamabad, he came to spend a couple of days with me and
took a room opposite mine in the hotel on the promise that we
would have all our meals together. When I went to his room in
the morning, he was drinking. I had my breakfast and left to
keep my appointments. When I returned at noon, he was
drinking. I had my lunch and retired for a siesta. Later in the

evening I joined him for a couple of drinks and had my dinner.
He continued drinking. His *mehfil* (party) went on till the early
hours of the morning. A rude piece of doggerel went as follows:

> *Faiz Ahmed Faiz say barh kar koee shaair nahin*
> *Jo chaman mein rah kar roz maarey veeraney ki gaand.*

(There is no better poet than Faiz Ahmed Faiz today
Who lives in a garden but buggers wilderness day after day.)

Faiz was unhappy with the way Punjabi-dominated Pakistan
treated its eastern wing, the way Bhutto manoeuvred to
deprive Sheikh Mujibur Rahman of the prime ministership of
the country and let loose General Tikka Khan's army on
hapless Bengalis. I went to see Bhutto in 1971 when he had
become head of state. After interviewing General Tikka Khan
I went to Faiz for dinner. Amongst his other guests was a pretty
girl who began needling me for meeting people like Bhutto and
Tikka Khan. I tried to explain to her that I was a journalist and
for me there were no good or bad guys only good or bad copy.
The argument got acrimonious. The girl sensed that Faiz did
not approve of her tone. She suddenly changed her manner.
'To make up for my nastiness I will sing for you,' she said. For
the next hour she sang Faiz's *ghazals in* her hauntingly
melodious voice. This was Nayyara whose recordings of these
songs have sold in the thousands.

Three years ago Urdu lovers the world over celebrated
Faiz's seventieth birthday. Faiz came to India and wherever he
went he received an enthusiastic welcome. People who could
not read Urdu knew his poems by heart and chanted them in
chorus as he recited them at their behest. It was not the
honours he received, not the Lenin Peace Prize, the Lotus
Award nor the honorary doctorates heaped on him but the love
of the man he was and the sort of poetry he wrote that

endeared him to millions of people of the subcontinent. He was the most lovable of men.

I have little doubt that Faiz had a premonition of his death. How else can anyone interpret the last poem that he wrote?

Ajal key haath koee aa rahaa hai parwaanah
Na jaaney aaj kee fehrist mein raqam kya hai.

(Death has some ordinance in its hand
I know not whose names are in its list today.)

Faiz's village of nativity, Kala Qadir, where he intended to spend his last days has renamed itself Faiz Nagar.

Faiz could not have asked for a better *imam zamin* for his journey into the ultimate.

G.S. FRASER: POETRY OF THE ADI GRANTH

How does one react when one learns that a friend of bygone days has been dead for some years? For a brief period of a month or so I met George Fraser every day and spent many hours pouring over manuscripts with him. He had been recommended as the reviser of translations of *The Sacred Writings of the Sikhs* initially rendered by a panel of Sikh scholars. I carried these translations to London and made the acquaintance of George Fraser who was a well-known literary critic and a minor poet. He turned out to be extremely shy, nervous, badly dressed and diffident to a degree I had not encountered before. He was forever lighting cigarettes, stubbing them out half-smoked and relighting them. One evening I took the Frasers to dinner with Manzur Qadir who was attending some conference as Pakistan's Foreign Minister. George was ill at ease in the presence of the dignitary and could hardly utter a word. Suddenly we smelt something burning and looked around to see if the carpet had caught fire. Fraser's wife knew what had happened: 'George, you've done it again!' she exclaimed. In his nervousness George had put his lighted cigarette in his trouser pocket.

For many months after we had finished the revision we kept up a desultory correspondence. He sent me a collection of his poems: I sent him a copy of *The Sacred Writings of the Sikhs* autographed by Dr Radhakrishnan who had written the introduction. Then we lost track of each other.

Last month I saw a review of a book entitled *A Stranger and Afraid: The Autobiography of an Intellectual* by G.S. Fraser. It was from that review that I learnt that George had been dead for three years. The title chosen by him encapsulated his personality. In one of his poems he wrote of his days at the university:

And in December on the ballroom floor
The girls in flowering dresses swayed and whirled,
And no girl leant on my protective arm,
From all the height of speculation hurled,
I stood and hesitated by the door.

If there was any way of honouring a dead man, the Sikh community owes that honour to George Fraser—perhaps a posthumous *siropa* (robe of honour) to be placed on his grave.

Incidentally, another man whose departure has gone unnoticed and who was the first to publish G.S. Fraser's poems in England was the Sri Lankan Tambimuttu.

Tambi, accompanied by his daughter, spent last winter in Delhi. He was full of plans for publishing works of Indian poets and writers in England. Last month he died in London and, like George Fraser, departed unhonoured and unsung.

A REQUIEM TO DOMSKY

I knew the father and the son, Frank and Dom Moraes, for most of their lives in India and England. Both had much in common. They were born in India. Both were Roman Catholics by birth but neither were practising Christians. Both had swarthy complexions as most Goans do but neither spoke a word of any Indian language: their mother tongue was English. Both handled the language with equal finesse—Frank as India's leading journalist of his times and Dom as a writer of lyrical prose and the best poet of the English language produced by India. Both were hard drinkers: the father died of cirrhosis of the liver, the son of cancer, no doubt caused by excessive drinking.

What undoubtedly hung like a dark cloud over their lives was the breakdown of a woman, Frank's wife and Dom's mother. She had to be sent to a mental asylum.

Dom's interest in poetry started very early in his life. Right from his first collection of poems *A Beginning* written when he was 19 and which won him the Hawthornden Prize for literature, whatever Dom wrote showed promise of greatness: two autobiographies, translations from Hebrew, several travelogues, covering Israel's wars against its neighbours, the trial and execution of the Nazi murderer Eichmann, all were highly readable. He was obsessed with death which haunted him like the ghost of his insane mother. He summed it up in memorable verse:

Death will be an interruption of my days
Of all matters pertinent to me
And the private intimacies I have that cannot be taken away
It will interrupt my talks with my dead father of
Moribund friends and bent, witchlike trees;
And most of all interrupt what I have with her
Who loves and saves me from my lost countries.

In his Preface to *Collected Poems: 1954-2004*, he wrote, 'I was about ten years old when I started to read poetry... I had an instinctive feel, even at that age, for the shape and texture of words.' By the time he was 12, he began to write it himself. He learnt French in order to be able to read Villon in the original. Poetry became a lifelong passion. But for a longish break (1965-1982), he continued to write till the end of his life. It would appear that the writer's block which had lasted 17 years was finally overcome when he met Sarayu Srivatsa to whom he dedicated this collection.

Dom Moraes is not easy to read. While his prose was limpid and lyrical, his poetry tended to be somewhat obscure as the works of many modern poets. His words have resonance but you have to read every line two or three times before you can comprehend their meaning. People brought up on simple rhyming verse like *Twinkle, twinkle, little star* will find Dom's poems elusive. Death was a recurrent theme as was his mother's insanity. The hawk was his symbol of doom. He sought escape from it in hard liquor and making love. He sums it up in *A Letter*:

My father hugging me so hard it hurt,
My mother mad, and time we went away.
We travelled, and I looked for love too young.
More travel, and I looked for lust instead.
I was not ruled by wanting: I was young,
And poems grew like maggots in my head.

I first met Dom when he joined Jesus College, Oxford. At the time, I was with the Indian High Commission in London and was living in Knightsbridge. Dom dropped in with Ved Mehta who was blind. He called him Domsky. So he became Domsky for all of us. They stayed on for drinks and dinner. Domsky was a chain-smoker—when the cigarette in his mouth was still half-smoked, he lit another one. He read out some of his poems. Before leaving he asked me if I would loan him £30. I did. A few days later his father sent me a cheque for £30. It became a pattern. The two boys would invite themselves over; Domsky would read out some of his poems, borrow some money which his father returned.

I met both boys many times. They came to my home in Delhi. Both wrote about me. Ved, despite his inability to see, gave a vivid description of my apartment, my long black beard and sparkling lecherous eyes as I stroked the thighs of an American girl with my family sitting around watching. Domsky portrayed me as a learned professor surrounded by books. Neither description had an iota of truth in it.

I saw more of Domsky than I did of Ved. Once Domsky brought over his blonde English lady friend with whom he sired a son. I saw more of Domsky after he married Leela Naidu who I had known when she was a schoolgirl in Paris, and later as the wife of one of the Oberois whom she bore twin daughters. Domsky and Leela were childhood friends and made for each other. I stayed with them in Hong Kong when he was editing R.V. Pandit's *Asia Magazine*. Pandit told me that once he barged into Domsky's office, opened the top drawer of his work desk, took out the bottle of Scotch and threw it out of the window. Pandit fought a losing battle with Domsky and had to finally fire him. The word 'discipline' did not exist in Domsky's dictionary.

Leela took me shopping in Hong Kong. Amongst the items that I had to buy were bras for my wife and daughter. Domsky wrote about it later alleging that being unable to indicate the sizes I required, I cupped my palms round bosoms of Chinese sales girls and asked for something larger. Domsky's imagination could run riot.

Back in Mumbai I got Domsky an assignment with the Dempos of Goa who were into shipping and mining. Domsky did a good book on Goa without a word on the Dempo family or their enterprises. I had to do a couple of pages to fill the gap. Later he got an assignment from the Madhya Pradesh government to do a book on its achievements. He wrote a lyrical account of the Madhya Pradesh countryside and his encounters with peasants and petty officials. The government had to add an appendix with facts and figures. I also came across a piece he wrote on Rajasthan for the American Embassy's monthly magazine *Span*. I have never read anything as beautifully worded as that piece.

Though Indian by birth and domicile, Domsky was as remote from being Indian as a Scottish Highlander. Once on Id-ul-Fitr, when Muslim worshippers spilled out of a mosque and offered *namaaz* in the streets, Domsky proceeded to walk through the serried ranks of *namaazis* to get to his home. He was badly roughed up.

Amongst the many assignments that came Domsky's way was writing the biography of Mrs. Indira Gandhi. Domsky and Leela met her on a regular basis. I asked Mrs. G (as he referred to her) how she communicated with Domsky who at the best of times mumbled *sotto voce*, barely audible. 'Leela translates everything for me,' she replied. The biography was published and presented to Mrs. G. A few days later Domsky and Leela went to call on her expecting to be thanked for doing a good job. Instead, Mrs. G snubbed them and walked out of the room in a huff. Mrs. G derived sadistic pleasure out of snubbing people she had befriended. Domsky and Leela were shattered.

Why Domsky broke up with Leela Naidu and picked up with Sarayu Srivatsa, I was never able to understand. By then he and I were barely on talking terms. David Davidar of Penguin Viking who had broached the subject with him told me that his response was typical of him: 'She has such a lovely bosom.'

With the arrival of Sarayu, he turned to writing on love but death remained a permanent fixture. We are not told how and when he fell in love with her. The confession is made in *Fourteen Years*:

> Fourteen years, the same mixture
> As when first I met her:
> ...Her breasts always ready:
> Mindmarks and handmarks on each other:
> I study the landscape of her body
> As architect, husband, and brother.

He confirms their love remained unabated.

> Under our feet the harsh subcontinent
> Where you and I were born,
> ...Eight years I have inhabited your weather,
> The clear and darker seasons of your mind.
> We have been more than married. It was meant.
> We've lived in each other. It was meant to be.

The last I saw of him and his companion was at the Writers' conference in Neemrana Fort. He looked much the same:

boyish face, ever smiling, glasses down the middle of his nose, cigarette dangling from his lips. Although I was not able to see much of her bosom, it struck me that Sarayu looked the epitome of a woman hundred per cent Indian. And Domsky's previous women had been white or half-European. Sarayu was also the only one who could match his skills as a writer. They did a couple of books together. He described her as 'my very closest, my harshest critic'.

Domsky was stricken with cancer but refused to undergo chemotherapy. He almost wallowed in the prospect of an early end with the ghost of his insane mother hovering over him.

> From a heavenly asylum, shrivelled Mummy,
> glare down like a gargoyle at your only son.
> ...That I'm terminally ill hasn't been much help.
> There is no reason left for anything to exist.
> Goodbye now. Don't try to meddle with this.

On the evening of Wednesday, 2 June 2004, Dom Moraes died in his sleep in Mumbai where he was born, lived, but never belonged.

KISHAN LAL: POETRY WITH *DAHI BHALLAS*

Kishan Lal probably came into my life more than ten years ago. I knew nothing about him till he told me he was the owner of Hotel Rajdoot on Mathura Road. Thereafter he came to see me twice every week. On both days he brought me food from the hotel: *dahi bhallas* for lunch and fish or chicken for dinner. In the afternoon, he would ring up and ask like any good restaurateur would, how I liked the food. The *dahi bhallas* are the best I have ever tasted: a judicious mix of yogurt with a couple of *bhallas*, with bananas, ginger, *saunth* and other condiments. I asked him why he always wanted to know how his food tasted. 'Because if you like something, I reward the cook. If you don't like something, I don't give him anything.' I made it a point to praise every item of food he gave me. The only other person he visited twice a week was Fali Nariman, who had been his lawyer and became a friend.

'You know I can't understand a word of what Kishan Lal says,' Nariman confessed to me. It was true. His speech was a mixture of mumbled gurgles. I had more trouble with it than Nariman as Kishan Lal had a passion for Urdu poetry, which he recited to me with great gusto. He would usually come up with one line and challenge me to come up with the next. I rarely passed his test. His favourite poet was Bahadur Shah Zafar.

Kishan Lal was not well conversant with English but hated to admit that he had difficulty with the language. He insisted I give him every book I wrote. On his next visit he would tell me triumphantly: 'I've got to page so-and-so. I must say you must have been a *rangeela*.'

Kishan Lal was a self-made man. He started life with a small coffee shop, went on to become military canteen contractor (amongst other, he served Lord Mountbatten) till he acquired land on Mathura Road and built Hotel Rajdoot. It acquired quite a reputation for its cuisine and risqué cabaret shows. It made Kishan Lal a millionaire: he acquired a farm and built himself a farmhouse.

Two years ago Kishan Lal had a fall and damaged one of his knees. Nevertheless, he kept up his bi-weekly visits. A few visits before the last one, he announced to me in English: 'I am 80.' Somehow 80 in English sounds something one can crow about while *'assee'* in Hindustani or *'ussean da'* in Punjabi has a tone of decline.

'You have another ten years to catch up with me,' I responded cheerfully. He threw his hands up in a gesture of despair and quoted lines from Zauq (oddly enough also my father's favourite):

Laaye hayaat, aaye qazaa,
Lay chalee chaley;
Apni khushee na aai hum,
Na apnee khushee chaley.

(Life came to me,
Death now stands at my door;
I came not of my pleasure,
I go not at my leisure.)

On the morning of Monday, 7 June 2004, my daughter called me in Kasauli from Delhi to say that somebody from Hotel Rajdoot had rung up to say that Lala Kishan Lal was dead and his cremation would take place that day.

That was not the end of Kishan Lal's story. A few days later after my column appeared I got a note from Fali Nariman which ran as follows:

'No more *dahi bhallas* for me till we meet again...'

'For me too, Khushwant—a beautiful touching piece. And Bapsi and I do miss his morning "gurgles".'

The Colombian novelist Gabriel Garcia Marquez has somewhere described a dream:

'In the early 1970s, I had an illuminating dream after living in Barcelona for five years. I dreamed I was attending my own funeral, walking with a group of friends dressed in solemn mourning but in a festive mood. We all seemed happy to be together. And I more than anyone else, because of the wonderful opportunity that death afforded me to be with my friends from Latin America, my oldest and dearest friends, the ones I had not seen for so long. At the end of the service, when they began to disperse, I attempted to leave too, but one of them made me see with decisive finality that as far as I was concerned, the party was over.

'"You are the only one that can't go," he said.

'Only then did I understand that dying means never being with friends again.'

That perhaps is the true sadness in Lalaji leaving us. For him, I am sure dying has meant never being with his friends again. We shall never know. But we do know that two of them fondly remember him and salute him. That may perhaps make him chuckle—and chuckling (as you will recall) always brought tears to his eyes!

The tribute to Kishan Lal yielded handsome dividends. His son Prem Mohan Kalra wrote to me saying that the bi-weekly of *dahi bhallas* would continue as during his father's lifetime:

Respected Sir,

For many years now whenever I sat beside my father I often heard of his trips to your house and furthermore, his friendly discussions with your good self; so much so that it reached a stage where we got to know you so well even without ever having the good fortune of meeting you. While my father was in the hospital during his last days, he would often ask me with great affection, 'Where is Sardar Khushwant Singhji these days?' And I would tell him that you were out of town. That would calm him for a while but he was not satisfied by my answer. He would then continue to ask if I had read your latest article.

Even in the ICU during his last two days, he asked us for a copy of The Hindustan Times *and would want me or my wife to read it out to him.*

I take this opportunity to thank you very sincerely with gratitude for having bestowed your affections and friendship upon my father. As per his instructions, all traditions initiated by him are to be carried out as they were being done during his lifetime. It will therefore be my humble effort to keep them going, and please let me have the honour of doing so as it will make Lalaji a very happy man in his heavenly abode. I would also be grateful if you could let me know if our dahi bhallas *taste as good as they used to during my father's time.*

I will definitely come and pay my respects in the near future as and when you permit me to do so.

With fondest regards and gratitude,

Prem Mohan Kalra
Son of Kishan Lal Kalra

YOGI BHAJAN: KHALSA FLAG
AT HALF MAST

Of the many godmen that it has been my privilege to meet, the one that I found most incomprehensible was Harbhajan Singh, popularly known as Yogi Bhajan. He died in his home in Espanola, New Mexico, USA on 7 October 2004 of heart failure at the age of 75.

Harbhajan was born on 26 August 1929 in a small town now in Pakistan. His father was a doctor. After Partition, the family migrated to India. He was schooled in Dalhousie. After graduating in Economics, he joined government service and was posted as a customs official at Palam Airport. Physical fitness, sports (hockey and football) were his abiding passions. With that, he also practised Yoga and became a master of Kundalini Yoga which he taught others. He came under a cloud and a department enquiry was instituted against him. Rather than face it, he migrated to Canada in 1968 and set up as a Yoga instructor in Toronto. From Toronto he moved to California in the US. He never looked back. Wherever he went, he taught an odd mixture of Sikhism and Kundalini Yoga. He called it 3HO—Healthy, Happy, Holy Organization. For some reason, he chose the fourth Guru Ramdas, the builder of

Amritsar, as his role model as a guru. The militant last Guru Gobind Singh who in fact established the Khalsa Panth did not figure prominently in Yogi's religious teaching. His 3HO Khalsas were pledged to vegetarianism. Soon a sect of Yogi Bhajan's American Sikhs evolved. They were distinctly white: men in white turbans, long flowing beards, kurta-pajama; women put their hair up in a bun and wrapped it round in white cloth. They took Sikh names with the suffix Khalsa attached to them. Within a few years, their numbers swelled to thousands. They set up gurdwaras of their own, learnt to recite the *Gurbani* and sing *keertan*. At times, Yogi brought his white disciples on chartered flights on pilgrimage to Punjab. Indian Sikhs were greatly flattered to see the message of their gurus taking root in foreign lands. Yogi, later given the honorific, Singh Sahib, was the first to plant the Khalsa flag on foreign soil.

Yogi Bhajan also had a keen eye for business. He made a killing in the health food industry. He opened a chain of vegetarian restaurants where only vegetables grown by organic manure were served. His Yogi Herbal Tea, based on Punjabi recipes, is about the tastiest and cold preventing as any that I have tasted. However, some of his products had amusing names: a chewing gum bears the name *Wahguru Choo*. His latest venture was to provide guards to the US government's high-security installations.

I met Yogi Bhajan at a dinner party especially organized for us to meet, in the home of multi-millionaire Nanak Kohli in Washington. He arrived with his entourage of Amazonian white lady disciples. I was surprised to see that a man who assiduously practised Yoga was pot-bellied. Also, one who practised the joys of simple living wore gold rings studded with precious stones on his fingers. He also had a voracious appetite: one of his Indian lady disciples brought his favourite *bhindi* (lady fingers) that she had cooked herself. He relished it. I had taken two American journalists on staff of *The Washington Post* with me, so that they could write something about his mission in life. They questioned him at some length. They were not impressed. He gifted me with a set of five books that he had written in Gurmukhi, as well as a gold miniature of the Sikh emblem Khanda-Kirpan.

Yogiji was an enigma. When fleeing from India, he borrowed Rs. 10,000 to pay for his air-ticket to Canada. Twenty years later when he was on one of his visits to India the daughter of the man from whom he had borrowed the money reminded him of the debt now owed to her. She expected to be paid back with interest because Yogiji was by now a very rich man. Instead of getting her father's money back, she got a snub. 'You are in your forties but are still caught in *maya jaal*—the web of illusion,' he said and blessed her.

No one can deny that Yogi Bhajan was Sikh religion's pioneer in the West. His going at 75, not a great age to go for a health-food faddist and a Yoga preacher, will be mourned by the Khalsa Panth by flying its flag at half mast for a long time to come.

How long Yogi Bhajan's legacy will last is hard to tell. He opened some schools and institutions in the US and Punjab. He leaves behind a wife, two sons and a daughter, none of whom shared his glory. He named no successor.

PROTIMA BEDI: SHE HAD A LUST FOR LIFE

Protima Gupta was born in Delhi in 1949. Her father, a small-time trader, was thrown out by his *Bania* father for marrying a dark, Bengali woman. He tried his luck in different cities of India, flopped everywhere and rejoined his family business. They had four children, three daughters and a son. Protima was their second daughter and the least loved. A loveless childhood turned her into a rebel. She was a bright girl and did well in her studies. Two words that were missing in her life's lexicon were 'no' and 'regret'; she could not say no to any man who desired her—and grew into a very desirable and highly animated young woman who most men found irresistible. And she did not regret any emotional or physical experience she had. She also felt that keeping secrets was like lying; so she told everyone everything, including her husband and succession of lovers who entered her life. She broke up marriages and remained blissfully unaware of the hurt she caused to people. She had to get everything off her chest. She told nothing but the truth about everyone she befriended. She might have added a few more chapters to her life story: why she abandoned her dance school and other business to become a *sanyasin,* but death took her unawares—she was killed in a landslide while on a pilgrimage to Kailash-Manasarovar on 18 August 1998. Oddly enough even as a *sanyasin* she was accompanied by one of her lovers. And on the same day in Bombay died Persis Khambatta, India's first beauty queen and one-time mistress of Protima's husband, Kabir Bedi.

I first met Protima in the home of Gopi Gauba in Bombay. Kabir, who I had known as a child in Lahore, was with her. I had little reason to like them as he had just ditched my friend B.C. Sanyal's daughter Amba to whom he was engaged and was living with Protima who was then only 19 years old. I did not exchange a word with either of them. When Protima became pregnant, they decided to get married. Pooja was their first child. But neither marriage nor having a child made either Protima or Kabir change their ways. While Kabir was away shooting some film with some starlet to keep him happy, Protima, mother of eight-month-old Pooja, was having an affair with a young German living next door. She was not sure if her son Siddhartha was from her husband or her pro-tem lover. She confessed her doubts to her husband and later told her son. The boy became a schizophrenic and later committed suicide in the USA.

Next I saw photographs of Protima running stark naked on a beach in Goa. It shocked middle-class society—exactly what she wanted to do. One day when I was editing *The Illustrated Weekly of India,* I.S. Jauhar asked me to come over with a photographer as he was getting engaged to Protima. On the phone I called him an ass, But I went. I published their photograph exchanging rings. That's all they wanted: pubicity. Protima later assured me that she had not as much as kissed Jauhar. I believed her because Protima never lied.

I did not see Protima blossom into an Odissi dancer. Nor did I see the dance village Nrityagram which she had created. She came to Bangalore to invite me. I accepted the invitation but when I discovered it would take me four hours on the road to get there and back, I called it off. She was very angry with me and swore she would never see me again. Her anger did not last long. When her son took his own life, she shaved off her long hair and renounced worldly pursuits. On her return to India she asked me to let her stay in my villa in Kasauli for a few days to be near Sanawar where her son had been at school for a short time. She spent four cold winter days walking about the hills all alone. She returned refreshed and full of smiles.

Protima Gauri (as she renamed herself) had zest for living. She loved her men, her liquor and drugs. She had a large range of lovers, most of whom she named. They include the singer Pandit Jasraj and the late Rajni Patel with whom she exchanged love letters till he was hospitalized and his wife Bakul forbade communication between them. Amongst the last was a businessman who abandoned his family and business to serve her.

It must have taken a lot of courage for her daughter Pooja to edit her mother's memoirs and decide to have them published. 'Passion, compassion and laughter,' writes Pooja were the three words which summed up her mother's personality in *Timepass: The Memoirs of Protima Bedi* (Viking, Penguin). Protima hated humbugs and hypocrites. She wrote, 'Every woman I knew secretly longed to have many lovers but she stopped herself for so many reasons. I had the capacity to love many at a time and for this had been called shallow and wayward and a good-time girl...'

I bless Protima for being the kind of person she was. I bless Pooja for letting us know what her mother had to say about herself. Many readers may be shocked at the revelations, many of her lovers who are still living and their wives and children will be acutely embarrassed by her disclosures but no one will be able to put down *Timepass* once he or she starts reading it.

NARGIS DUTT: MOTHER INDIA

For many years the picture of Nargis troubled my midnights, and my noon reposes. She remained a lovely, distant apparition beyond the approach of earthly mortals like me. Then one morning my telephone rang and a dulcet voice announced: 'This is Nargis Dutt speaking. Can I speak to Mr. so-&-so?'

'It is so-&-so speaking. Would you by any means be Nargis the film star?'

'Jee-haan.'

'*Mother India* and all that?'

'Jee-haan. Can I come and see you?'

An hour later, she breezed into my office setting many a heart wildly aflutter. She was as beautiful as she was unassuming and friendly. 'I have come to ask you for a personal favour,' she said. 'I believe you have a house in Kasauli. My children are at Sanawar and I can't find anywhere to stay during the school Founder's Week celebrations. I was wondering if you could let me stay in your house.'

'Of course!' I replied. 'But only on one condition.' I paused to create the necessary suspense. She looked quizzically at me: 'What?'

'Provided thereafter I have your permission to tell anyone I like that Nargis slept in my bed.'

She burst into peals of girlish laughter. 'Done!' she said, putting out her hand to make a compact. 'I stay in your house; you say I slept in your bed.'

Nargis repeated this dialogue many times without the slightest embarrassment. She had the knack of making people happy. And a malicious sense of humour. But the last time she was in Delhi to attend the session of the Rajya Sabha, she was somewhat lacking in her usual exuberance. 'I shouldn't be here. My doctor told me I have some kind of jaundice. I promised the local Rotary I would come—I couldn't break my word, could I? And there is this debate on Baghpat.'

The debate, as you might recall, was largely the tirade let loose by the Opposition on the shooting of three men and the alleged rape of Maya Tyagi in the police station. The atmosphere in the House was surcharged with emotion. A lady member somewhat dark and corpulent exploded a volcano of angry epithets, pouring lava on the government which though headed by a woman allowed women to be insulted, molested and raped. 'There is a rape here and a rape there! Every day we hear of rape, rape, rape,' she shrilled. Nargis who was sitting next to me became suddenly very animated. 'Why are you getting so excited?' she shouted. 'No one will ever rape you.' Mercifully, only a few members sitting near her heard her remark and laughed jovially.

Nargis was very sick. I tried to see her in New York. The receptionist at the Sloane-Kettering was not impressed by my telling her that I had come across half the world to see her. 'Are you her husband?' she demanded somewhat exasperated at my insistence.

'Alas no,' I replied, 'only a distant friend and an ardent admirer.'

So Nargis is gone. I for one had never believed that she had been discharged from Sloane-Kettering as cured; they were of the opinion that nothing more could be done for her and she decided to come home to die.

> Now boast thee, death, in possession lies
> A lass unparalleled.

Beautiful she was in all senses of the word. Shaped in classic mould enshrining a heart of gold which went out to the poor, the blind and the paraplegic. Her smile was bewitching, her laughter contagious. She had the gift of eternal youth and died looking as young in her fifties as she had in her teens.

One thing that intrigued me was her faith. Was she Muslim or Hindu or both or nothing? She wore a bindi on her forehead, married a Brahmin, gave her children Hindu names and was often seen in Swami Muktanand's ashram at Ganeshpuri. Nevertheless, she was buried with Muslim rites in a Muslim graveyard with her Hindu husband reciting the *fateha* (prayer). I can't think of any Indian family which better exemplified the principle of *Sarva Dharma Samabhav* (equal respect for all faiths).

My chief claim to fame as a Member of the Rajya Sabha was that I sat next to Nargis and was the envy of my brother parliamentarians. That seat has remained unoccupied since last August. No doubt someone else will be nominated to fill her place. But the void she leaves in the hearts of millions of her countrymen will never be filled.

AMRITA SHERGIL: *FEMME FATALE*

I am hardly justified in describing Amrita Shergil as a woman in my life. I met her only twice. But these two meetings remain imprinted in my memory. Her fame as an artist, her glamour as a woman of great beauty which she gave credence to in some of her self-portraits, and her reputation for promiscuity snowballed into a veritable avalanche which hasn't ended to this day and gives me an excuse to include her in my list.

One summer, her last, I heard that she and her Hungarian cousin-husband who was a doctor had taken an apartment across the road where I lived in Lahore. He meant to set up a medical practice; she, her painting studio. Why they chose to make their home in Lahore, I have no idea. She had a large number of friends and admirers in the city. She also had rich, landowning relatives on her Sikh father's side who regularly visited Lahore. It seemed as good a place for them to start their lives as any in India.

It was June 1941. My wife had taken our seven-month-old son, Rahul, for the summer to my parents' house 'Sunderban' in Mashobra, seven miles beyond Shimla. I spent my mornings at the High Court gossiping with lawyers over cups of coffee or listening to cases being argued before judges. I had hardly any case to handle myself. Nevertheless, I made it a point to wear my black coat, white tabs around the collar and carry my black gown with me to give others an appearance of being very busy. I returned home for lunch and a long siesta before I went to play tennis at the Cosmopolitan Club.

One afternoon I came home to find my flat full of the fragrance of expensive French perfume. On the table in my sitting room-cum-library was a silver tankard of chilled beer. I tiptoed to the kitchen, asked my cook about the visitor. 'A memsahib in a sari,' he informed me. He had told her I would be back any moment for lunch. She had helped herself to a bottle of beer from the fridge and was in the bathroom freshening up. I had little doubt my uninvited visitor was none other than Amrita Shergil.

For several weeks before her arrival in Lahore I had heard stories of her exploits during her previous visits to the city before she had married her cousin. She usually stayed in Faletti's Hotel. She was said to have made appointments with her lovers with two-hour intervals—at times six to seven a day—before she retired for the night. If this was true (men's gossip is less reliable than women's) love formed very little part of Amrita's life. Sex was what mattered to her. She was a genuine case of nymphomania, and according to her nephew Vivan Sundaram's published account, she was also a lesbian. Her *modus vivendi* is vividly described by Badruddin Tyabji in his memoirs. One winter when he was staying in Shimla, he invited Amrita to dinner. He had a fire lit for protection from cold and Western classical music playing on his gramophone. He wasted the first evening talking of literature and music. He invited her again. He had the same log fire and the same music. Before he knew what was happening, Amrita simply took her clothes off and lay stark naked on the carpet. She did

not believe in wasting time. Even the very proper Badruddin
Tyabji got the message.

Years later Malcolm Muggeridge, the celebrated author,
told me that he had spent a week in Amrita's parents' home in
Summer Hill, Shimla. He was then in the prime of his youth—
his early twenties. In a week she had reduced him to a rag. 'I
could not cope with her,' he admitted. 'I was glad to get back
to Calcutta.'

A woman with the kind of reputation Amrita enjoyed drew
men towards her like iron filings to a magnet. I was no
exception. As she entered the room, I stood up to greet her.
'You must be Amrita Shergil,' I said. She nodded. Without
apologizing for helping herself to my beer she proceeded to tell
me why she had come to see me. They were mundane matters
which robbed our first meeting of all romance. She wanted to
know about plumbers, dhobis, carpenters, cooks, bearers, etc.,
in the neighbourhood whom she could hire. While she talked
I had a good look at her. Short, sallow-complexioned, black
hair severely parted in the middle, thick sensual lips covered in
bright red lipstick, stubby nose with blackheads visible. She
was passably good looking but by no means a beauty.

Her self-portraits were exercises in narcissism. She
probably had as nice a figure as she portrayed herself in her
nudes but I had no means of knowing what she concealed
beneath her sari. What I can't forget is her brashness. After she
had finished talking, she looked around the room. I pointed to
a few paintings and said, 'These are by my wife; she is an
amateur.' She glanced at them and scoffed, 'That is obvious.' I
was taken aback by her disdain but did not know how to retort.
More was to come.

A few weeks later I joined my family in Mashobra. Amrita
was staying with the Chaman Lals who had rented a house
above my father's. I invited them for lunch. The three of
them—Chaman, his wife Helen and Amrita, came at midday.

The lunch table and chairs were lined on a platform under the shade of a holly oak which overlooked the hillside and a vast valley. My seven-month-old son was in the playpen teaching himself how to stand up on his feet. He was a lovely child with curly brown locks and large questioning eyes. Everyone took turns to talk to him and compliment my wife for producing such a beautiful boy. Amrita remained lost in the depths of her beer mug. When everyone had finished, she gave the child a long look and remarked, 'What an ugly little boy!' Everyone froze. Some protested at the unkind remark. But Amrita was back to drinking her beer. After our guests had departed, my wife said to me very firmly, 'I am not having that bloody bitch in my house again.'

Amrita's bad behaviour became the talk of Shimla's social circle. So did my wife's comment on her. Amrita got to know what my wife had said and told people, 'I will teach that bloody woman a lesson she won't forget; I will seduce her husband.'

I eagerly awaited the day of seduction. It never came. We were back in Lahore in autumn. So were Amrita and her husband. One night her cousin Gurcharan Singh (Channi) who owned a large orange orchard near Gujranwala turned up and asked if he could spend the night with us, as Amrita, who had asked him over for the weekend, was too ill to have him stay with her. The next day, other friends of Amrita's dropped in. They told us that Amrita was in a coma and her parents were coming down from Summer Hill to be with her. She was an avid bridge player and in her semi-conscious moments mumbled bridge calls. The next morning I heard that Amrita was dead.

I hurried to her apartment. Her father, Sardar Umrao Singh Shergil, stood by the door in a daze, mumbling a prayer. Her Hungarian mother went in and out of the room where her daughter lay dead unable to comprehend what had happened. That afternoon no more than a dozen men and women followed Amrita's cortège to the cremation ground. Her husband lit her funeral pyre. When we returned to her apartment, the police were waiting for her husband. Britain had declared war on Hungary as an ally of its enemy, Nazi Germany. Amrita's husband was therefore considered an enemy because of his nationality, and had to be detained in prison.

He was lucky to be in police custody. A few days later, his mother-in-law, Amrita's mother, started a campaign against him accusing him of murdering her daughter. She sent letters to everyone she knew asking for a full investigation into the circumstances of her daughter's sudden death. I was one of those she sent a letter to. Murder it certainly was not; negligence, perhaps. I got details from Dr Raghubir Singh who was our family doctor and the last person to see Amrita alive. He told me that he had been summoned at midnight. Amrita had peritonitis caused perhaps by a clumsy abortion. She had bled profusely. Her husband asked Dr Raghubir Singh to give her blood transfusion. The doctor refused to do so without fully examining his patient. While the two doctors were arguing with each other, Amrita quietly slipped out of life. But her fame liveth evermore.

CHETAN ANAND: ON LOSING A FRIEND

For many years we were the closest of friends. Our jobs took us to distant cities. Nevertheless, we remained in constant touch. The closeness lasted for over thirty years. Then he turned indifferent and I felt hurt. He was one of the people I wrote about in my *Women and Men in My Life*. He was hurt by what I had to say about him. That had not been my intention. Nevertheless, when I heard of his death on the morning of Sunday, 6 July 1997, I was overcome with remorse and sorrow. Our past association haunted me for several days and nights.

Our friendship began in 1932 when we found ourselves in the same class in Government College, Lahore, studying the same subjects and living in the same hostel. Chetan was a very pretty boy: fair, with curly hair and dreamy eyes.

He started seeking my company more to protect himself, and not so much because he shared common interests with me. We ate our breakfasts together, attended classes together, played tennis in the afternoons and at least twice a week, went to the movies. During vacations he went home to Gurdaspur. We wrote to each other. He was into writing poetry à la Gurudev Tagore. He sent his compositions to me. Soppy stuff, but I was flattered.

Chetan had to count his rupees. One year he put himself up for election for the secretaryship of the Hindu-Sikh dining room, and, as was the custom those days, had cards printed soliciting votes. I could not understand why anyone would want to oversee cooking and feeding arrangements in a college hostel mess. I discovered that catering contractors bestowed extra favours to secretaries by not charging them for meals. The elections were as fiercely contested as those of the college union. Chetan won.

After we passed out of college we found ourselves together in London. I was studying law; he came to take a shot at the ICS. We both took the examination. Neither of us made the grade. Chetan could not afford to stay on in England and returned home.

We resumed our friendship when I came back to Delhi. He and Iqbal Singh were the only two friends I invited to my wedding in October 1939. A year later, when I set up practice in Lahore, Chetan spent many months of the summer in my flat. Though till then he had not found a job, he was highly successful in winning the favours of young ladies. His technique was simple. On hot June afternoons he would go in his overcoat carrying a single rose in his hand. When the recipient of the rose asked him why he was wearing an overcoat, he would answer, 'Because it is the only thing I possess in the world.'

One who fell heavily for this approach was the ravishing Uma, daughter of Professor Chatterjee. We celebrated their engagement in my apartment. That very evening I caught him flirting with another girl. He was never a one-woman man. Uma married him, had two sons and then left him to become Ebrahim Alkazi's second wife. Chetan shifted to Bombay to try his luck in films. There he shacked up with Priya, a good twenty years younger than him. He did his best to turn her into a film star. He did not succeed.

Chetan did not make his mark as a director or an actor as his obituaries now claim. He made one good film *Neecha Nagar*; the rest were second-rate, and earned him neither fame nor money. He did an excellent job reproducing the light and sound show at the Red Fort in Delhi for which I had written the master script in 1965. He got assignments from the Punjab government which he was unable to fulfil.

It was not his successes or failures in films that affected my affection for him; it was his indifference towards me when I moved to Bombay to take up the editorship of *The Illustrated Weekly of India* in 1969. I was there for a whole nine years and expected to see a lot of Chetan. I saw something of my other college friends: Balraj Sahni, B.R. Chopra, Kamini Kaushal and even Chetan's own brother Dev Anand. But Chetan, with whom I looked forward to resuming my close friendship, did not bother to contact me even once. Only a month or so before I left Bombay I ran into him and his lady friend at a party. Very airily he said, '*Oi Sardar! Tu milta hee nahin*—O Sardar! You never meet me.' I exploded with anger, '*Besharam!* You shameless creature! Is this the way you fulfil obligations of a forty-year-old friendship?'

His lady friend tried to protest and invited me to come over. 'I don't want to set foot in your home or see this fellow's face again,' I replied and stormed out.

Now I regret what I said as I recall Chetan with tears in my eyes.

DHARMA KUMAR: WOMEN LIKE HER
DO NOT DIE...

She died early morning on Friday, 19 October 2001. She was in the intensive care of Apollo Hospital for over a month; so her end did not come as a surprise. What sustained a little hope in my mind was that women like Dharma did not die; they faded out of memory like a lost dream. She was 73. I would add the word 'only' to the sentence because she seemed agelessly youthful. She was more animated than any woman I have ever met. I write about her because all of us have someone or the other in our lives who means more to us than we care to admit till after they are gone.

It must be over 50 years ago when I first met her and her husband Lavraj Kumar at a large luncheon party in a garden. He was an executive in Burma Shell; she was working on her doctoral thesis for Cambridge University. She was the centre of attraction, sparkling with wit and humour and mimicking celebrities. She had everyone in splits of happy laughter. I was completely bowled over. For the next few days I spoke about her to everyone I knew and tried to get as much information about her and her husband as I could.

Lavraj Kumar was from Uttar Pradesh, the only child of well-known and rich parents. He was also a very bright

student. He won a Rhodes scholarship to Oxford. Dharma was
a Tamilian Brahmin and the only child of a well-known
scientist, Dr Venkatraman, who was the head of the National
Chemical Laboratory in Pune. They met in England and got
married. Lavraj answered all that Dharma wanted of a man.
She had exaggerated respect for academics; almost all her
cousins had gained firsts in Oxford or Cambridge; Lavraj had
bettered them. She did not much care for wealth. She married
him because he was brighter than any other of her many
suitors. She, however, did not like Lavraj joining Burma Shell,
becoming a *boxwallah* and taking orders from White *sahibs*.
Lavraj was a soft-spoken and self-effacing man. Dharma was
outgoing, garrulous and revelled in admiration. She was not
the kind of woman I usually fell for. Her features were
passable; she used no make-up or perfume. It was her
animation which I found irresistible. Her legs and hands were
never still. Her eyes sparkled as she spoke. Come to think of
it, the only reason she responded to my overtures was that she
was overwhelmed by my adoration. It was an entirely one-
sided affair. I dedicated my second novel *I Shall Not Hear The
Nightingale* to her. I don't think she bothered to read it.

Her favourite put-downers were about a cousin Raghavan
Aiyar. Like others of the family, he was a topper: first in MA
Philosophy from Madras; first class first in Cambridge and
elected President of the Cambridge Union. While in the
university, he acquired a group of admirers who assembled in
his room periodically to hear him speak. He told them that the
source of all human frailties was the ego. Unless one
conquered one's ego, there could be no peace of mind. One
day a lady admirer asked, 'I agree with all you say about the
ego, but how does one conquer the ego?'

'Good question!' replied Raghavan Aiyar. 'You will
appreciate it poses a bigger problem for me than it does for
you. For myself I have evolved a formula for self-extinction.

Everyday I sit in *padmasana* (lotus pose), shut my eyes and repeat: "I am not the Raghavan Aiyar who got a first class from Madras University; I am not the Raghavan Aiyar who got a first class first from Cambridge University; I am not the Raghavan Aiyar who is the most brilliant philosopher of the East; I am merely a vehicle of the mahatmas, a spark of the Divine."'

According to Dharma when Raghavan Aiyar stood for presidentship of the union, he did not bother to canvass for himself but left it to his admirers. After the counting of votes, his fans rushed to his room to break the good news. They found him seated in *padmasana* on his carpet with his eyes shut: 'You've won: You've won!' they shouted triumphantly. Raghavan Aiyar raised one hand with his finger pointing to the roof and exclaimed: 'Victory is Thine O' Lord!'

Dharma got her doctorate in Economics. She became a Professor in Delhi School of Economics and wrote a couple of books which were very well received by economists. Her husband left Burma Shell to become Secretary in the Petroleum Ministry of the Central Government. She was happy that she was no longer the wife of a *boxwallah*. But even as the wife of a much-respected bureaucrat, she refused to entertain ministers or befriend their wives. When compelled to meet them, because of her husband's status, she would go out of her way to belittle them.

Undeterred by her indifference, I continued to long for her company. The break came unexpectedly. Lavraj had invited her closest friends for dinner to celebrate her invitation for a lecture tour abroad. Very light-heartedly I asked, 'Dharma, how did you wangle it?' She went pale with anger and burst out: 'I don't like that kind of insinuation. I am not a wangler.' The outburst of anger took everyone unawares. An uneasy silence descended. The party was ruined.

The one thing I could not forgive or forget is people losing their temper with me. I swore to have nothing more to do with

Dharma. She was the victim of uncontrollable temper, I of being unable to forgive. She did her best to make amends but something within me had snapped which I could not join together.

After some months, our families began to see each other again. But I was never relaxed in her company. I transferred my affection to her husband and even more to her daughter Radha.

When her husband died suddenly, I went to the crematorium, expecting to meet Dharma and wipe out the uneasiness that had come between us. She was not there. I condoled with Radha and Lavraj's uncle Dharamvira (former Governor of Punjab and Bengal). I told him, 'Dharma had all the gifts anyone would wish for except the gift of friendship.' He agreed with me.

None of us who cherished Dharma realized that her fits of temper may have been due to things going wrong inside her. She developed a brain tumour and had to be flown to London for surgery. It did not help. Another tumour developed. Then another. Dharamvira was dead; her friends had deserted her. The only one left to look after her was her 94-year-old mother-in-law. She told everyone, 'Dharma is not my *bahu* (daughter-in-law) but my *beti* (daughter).'

She was with her to the last.

It is hard for me to accept the fact that Dharma was mortal. I will not see Dharma any more. She may not have cared for me but I will cherish her memory for the years left to me.

P.C. LAL: AIR CHIEF MARSHAL

W hat's happened to the Basant Lals?' My 87-year-old
mother asked one morning. I told her what I knew and
asked: 'What made you suddenly think of the Basant Lals after
all these years?'

'I don't know,' she replied, 'but all morning I've been
thinking about them. Didn't the elder boy become somebody
very big in the aeroplane business, like our Arjun? What is his
name?'

'Pratap! He succeeded Arjun as the Air Chief Marshal.'

Strange coincidence that at the time my mother was
making enquiries about the Basant Lals in Delhi, Pratap was
dying in London.

Our families had been very close to each other; the
closeness survived three generations. Pratap was six when he
joined our class in Modern School. My almost day-to-day
association with him lasted sixty years. At school we exchanged
turbans. My intentions were not very honest as my juvenile
mind was more preoccupied by his sister, Roma, than my
dharambhai (brother of the same faith).

If there was anyone who disproved the Hindi proverb

'*Honhar birwan ke hot chikne paat*'—a child of promise bears
marks of future greatness—it was Pratap Chandra Lal. He was
a poor student and he hated games. He was timid and lacking
in self-confidence. He could never make up his mind about
what he wanted to be. However, while at school he got his
flying licence—something unheard of those days.

After school, Pratap joined me at King's College in London
and the Inns of Court. He finished neither course of study but
succeeded in placing articles in the prestigious *Manchester
Guardian*. We spent our holidays together. What gave him
malicious pleasure was that wherever we stayed, I was taken to
be his father: to pre-empt my pleading that we were about the
same age, he would deliberately address me as 'Pop'. Amongst
my prized possessions are several letters he wrote to a girl both
of us were then courting giving descriptions of the countryside
liberally interspersed with caricatures of me without my
turban. The letters formed a valuable part of the dowry of the
girl when she married me. I often tormented Pratap by quoting
from them.

After a short stint as a journalist, Pratap joined the Air
Force. It was by these fortuitous circumstances that he
stumbled into the career for which he was best suited.

The real change in Pratap's personality came after he
married Hashi. He gained self-assurance, became an ace flier,
a man of enormous rectitude and courage, the like of which
has become all too rare today. Once leading an IAF team to
inspect aircraft in England he had to confront the very prickly
Krishna Menon. Menon had placed orders for a particular kind
of aircraft and wanted the IAF team to put their thumb
impression on the deal. Lal not only refused to do so but put
in writing that the machines were unsuitable and not available
in the numbers required at the time. Menon was furious and
not knowing what to do, accused Lal of having been bribed by
a rival firm. Lal stood his ground with the supreme confidence

that goes with a man whose conscience is crystal clear. It later transpired that it was not Lal but Menon who had been bribed.

When Menon became Minister of Defence, Lal had to suffer working under him. He was transferred to Hindustan Aeronautics Ltd. simply to put him out of the running for the top post in the IAF. It was only after Menon fell from grace that Pratap was brought back to the Air Force and in due course became its chief.

The air operations in the 1971 war against Pakistan were masterminded by Lal. It was his strategy that knocked out the teeth of the Pakistani Air Force in Bangladesh. Within a few hours of the declaration of the war, the Dacca and Chittagong airstrips were rendered unserviceable; the Pakistani Air Force mess next to Dacca airport was knocked out by a direct hit and the Governor cowed to submission by a hail of bullets fired into the windows of his residence. I recall ringing up Lal from Bombay to tell him that some British and American papers had written that the Pakistani Air Force had got the better of the Indian on the western front. He was indignant. 'Rubbish! I will prove to you by concrete evidence that our boys gave them more in return than they received.' And so he did with figures and photographs.

Another trait that none of his contemporaries had suspected in Lal was efficiency and hard work. The way he streamlined the functioning of Air India and Indian Airlines, refusing doggedly to give in to arm-twisting by the pilots' union, earned him a deserved reputation as a first-class administrator.

Lal was a magnanimous man. He was removed from his post of Chairman of Air India and Indian Airlines by Sanjay Gandhi and took a job with the Tatas. When Sanjay fell from power and most people avoided meeting members of the Gandhi family, I had to go to Calcutta to appear as a co-accused with Maneka Gandhi in a case against *Surya*. I was staying with the Lals; Maneka with Kamal Nath.

'The Lals must hate us,' I recall Maneka telling me. Lal hated no one. It was Hashi who invited Maneka over to their house and instead of showing any resentment against what had been done to them, treated her with great courtesy and affection.

Pratap was a very conventional home-loving type. He was as abstemious as a Jain monk: a non-smoker, non-drinker (I had to extract my drinks from him) and prudishly Victorian. He disapproved of the use of four-letter words and blushed every time I used them. He had strong views about propriety in dress and deportment and disapproved of girls wearing tight-fitting clothes or shirts. He was a square in every sense of the word. Despite the gulf that divided us in our professions and our views, he was amongst the few I learnt to respect, admire and cherish.

And that for the simple reason that P.C. Lal was a perfect gentleman.

JACK WILBERFORCE BURKE PEEL: MY ENGLISH BHAI

His name will mean nothing to my readers. It meant a great deal to me. He was my closest English friend for over 70 years. He died on the 3 April 2004 at the age of 95. I read of it in *The Independent* (London). It was a two-column obituary with his photograph.

Despite my closeness to him I did not realize his greatness as like most Englishman of breeding he never spoke about himself. It was from the obituary I learnt that Jack Peel in his time had met Stalin, Tito, Eisenhower, Churchill, Attlee and many other world figures and helped them to communicate with each other. He was not a politician, minister of government or a diplomat; he was a humble clerk with a gift for languages. He was fluent in half-dozen European languages and spoke with the fluency he spoke his native English. Although he never went to a university, he was widely read and an accomplished pianist.

I met him when I was a student and had taken lodging with Professor F.S. Marvin in Welwyn Garden City some 40 miles north of London. Our first encounter was on the tennis courts in an inter-club tournament. He was better at the game than I.

Gradually a friendship developed and I was invited over for tea to meet his father who ran a small private school, his sister Nancy and his wife, a very pretty Estonian girl named Dagmar Hansen. We often found ourselves travelling together in the same train from Welwyn Garden City to King's Cross station, morning and evening. I recall him telling me once, 'I don't have much reason to befriend a Sikh. The last time I made friends with one, he walked off with my girlfriend. His name was Gurdial Singh. He was in the Indian Air Force doing some kind of course at Hatfield. Do you know him?' I had not heard of Gurdial Singh, I replied, 'You better beware of all Sikhs; you have a very pretty wife.'

On days I had no college, I often dropped in a café to have a cup of coffee because Dagmar worked there as a waitress. Jack had a clerical job in the London branch of the National Bank of India and their home needed two incomes. Dagmar spoke very little English. I suspected that apart from her looks Jack had married her to keep his knowledge of the languages she spoke: Estonian, Russian and German. He was a quick learner. By the time World War II broke out, he had full command of these languages.

In 1943 the Royal Air Force took him on its staff to monitor what passed between pilots of the German Luftwaffe carrying out air raids over Britain. The authorities soon found that Jack was as fluent in Russian as he was in German. So he was made a liaison officer in a department handling Soviet pilots training to handle British air fighters. He became an interpreter for the Soviet minister Vyacheslav Molotov and with the Soviet Ambassador Ivan Maisky. He was seconded to the British Foreign Service and posted as Second Secretary in the British Embassy in Moscow. There he met Josef Stalin. Unlike the popular image of Stalin as a cold-blooded dictator of little learning, Jack found him to be a warm, fatherly figure with a sharp memory. His English colleagues who looked down on

him as an upstart tried to cut him down to size by asking him
to play a piano piece by Prokofiev at an embassy reception.
Jack did it, with panache unaware that the composer was
standing behind him.

Jack resigned from his Moscow job in 1947 to return to
Welwyn Garden City to be close to his wife who was seriously
ill with tuberculosis. She died in 1947 leaving behind a son.

I lost track of Jack Peel during the war years. But no sooner
it ended and I found myself a job in India House, London, I
resumed contact with him. By then I had a wife
and two children. Jack was a widower. He held a senior
position in the Imperial Chemical Industries and because of
his mastery over various languages, put in charge of their
operations in Eastern Europe. Largely because of him I shifted
my family from London to Welwyn Garden City. We met
almost every day. Instead of tennis we played squash at
lunchtime and followed that up with tankards of beer and
sandwiches in a nearby pub. As in the past, we often travelled
in the same train from Welwyn Garden City to King's Cross
and back.

I quit the service in 1951 and returned to India.

We wrote to each other. The same year Jack married an
Austrian girl Erika Fischa through whom he had another two
sons. One winter they came to Delhi and stayed with us. He
had then developed an arthritic knee and walked with a limp.
Whenever I needed medicines not available in India—as I did
when my father and later my mother were taken ill—I could
rely on Jack to send them without doctors' prescriptions which
were mandatory. He kept track of my ventures into the writing
world by getting my books and writing to me about them.
Besides languages and classical music he had an abiding
interest in literature from his school days in Scarborough
(Yorkshire). The Sitweil family Edith, Osbert and Sacheverell
were family friends.

During the last few years instead of Jack it was his wife Erika who responded to my letters. When my wife died in 2002, Erika wrote to me; Jack added a paragraph at the end of the letter. I was barely able to decipher it.

Erika's last letter to me was about Jack's rapidly declining health. He was confined to his bed but he added three words to his wife's letter. It took me some time to decipher them: 'How are you?'

MANZUR QADIR: THE ROLE MODEL

My closest friend of many years lay dying; I could not go to his bedside. His wife and children were only an hour-and-a-half's flight from me; I could not go to see them. I could not ring them up nor write to them. And when he died, I was not there to comfort them. They are Pakistani, I am Indian. What kind of neighbours are we? What right have we to call ourselves civilized?

I had missed the news in the morning paper. When a friend rang me up and said, 'Your old friend is gone,' the blood in my veins froze. I picked up the paper from the wastepaper basket and saw it in black and white. Manzur Qadir was dead. At the time he was dying in London, I was drinking and listening to Vividh Bharati in Bombay. And when he was being laid to rest in the family graveyard at Lahore, I was wringing my hands in despair in Colaba. He was Pakistani, I am Indian.

It is believed that when a person is dying, all the events of his life flash before his mind's eye. I must have occupied many precious seconds of Manzur Qadir's dying thoughts as he also regarded me as his closest friend. I spent the whole morning thinking of how we met and why I was drawn close to him. At our first meeting thirty years ago we had talked about death. I had quoted lines from the last letter his wife Asghari's brother had written to his father, Mian Fazl-i-Husain:

I am working by candlelight,
It flickers, it's gone.

Manzur Qadir was a man of contradictions. He showed little promise as a student; he became the most outstanding lawyer of Pakistan. Next to law, his favourite reading was the Old Testament and the *Koran*. Nevertheless he remained an agnostic to the very last. He was an uncommonly good poet and wrote some of the wittiest, bawdiest verse known in the Urdu language. At the same time he was extremely conservative, correct in his speech and deportment. Although born a Punjabi he rarely spoke the language and preferred to converse in Hindustani which he did with uncommon elegance. He was long-winded but never a bore; a teetotaller who effervesced like vintage champagne.

The dominant traits of his character were kindliness—he never said a hurtful word about anyone. And integrity which surpassed belief. He made upwards of Rs 50,000 a month; income-tax authorities were constantly refunding tax he had paid in excess. He did not give a tinker's cuss about money. It was commonly said, 'God may lie, but not Manzur Qadir.' Though godless he had more goodness in him than a clutch of saints.

The respect and admiration he commanded amongst his friends was unparalleled. Some years after Partition a group of us were discussing G.D. Khosla's *Stern Reckoning*. The book, as the title signifies, justified the killings that took place in East Punjab in the wake of Partition as legitimate retribution. We were going for Khosla's partisan approach; he and his wife were arguing back. Suddenly a friend asked Khosla, 'Would

you present a copy of this book to Manzur?' Khosla pondered
for a while and replied, 'No, not to him.' That ended the
argument. We came to judge the right or wrong of our actions
by how Manzur Qadir would react. He was the human
touchstone of our moral pretensions.

Manzur Qadir had no interest in politics and seldom
bothered to read newspapers. His ignorance of world affairs
was abysmal. Once in London we happened to see a newsreel
of Dr Sun Yat Sen. He asked me who this Sen was. When I
expressed my amazement at his lack of information, he
retorted testily: 'Hoga koee sala Bangali daktar.' Later in the
evening, when I narrated the incident to his daughter Shireen,
she chided her father. He made me swear I wouldn't tell
anyone about it. I didn't till I read in the papers that President
Ayub Khan had made him Foreign Minister of Pakistan. I sent
him a telegram of congratulations, 'Greetings from, Dr Sun Yat
Sen, the Bengali doctor.'

I spent a short holiday with him when he was Foreign
Minister. I stayed as a guest in my own home. (I had put him
in possession when I left Lahore in August 1947. He not only
saved the life of my Sikh servants whom he brought to the
Indian border at night at considerable risk to his life, but sent
back every book in my library, every item of furniture and even
the remains of liquor in my drink cabinet.) He told me how he
had become Foreign Minister. He had criticized Ayub Khan's
dictatorship at a meeting. That evening an army jeep came to
fetch him. Believing that he was being arrested he said good-
bye to his family. He was driven to the President's residence.
Said Ayub Khan: 'It is no good criticizing me and my
government unless you are willing to take the responsibility for
what you say.' Manzur Qadir returned home as Foreign
Minister.

True to his character, Manzur never canvassed for any job
nor showed the slightest eagerness to hold on to power. He

strove with none, for none was worth his strife. He allowed himself to be outmanoeuvred by unscrupulous politicians. After four years as Foreign Minister, during which he made a desperate bid to improve relations with India, he quit the job with no regrets. He was forced to become Chief Justice and, when he desired to throw that up, persuaded to take up briefs on behalf of the government. He was engaged as government counsel in all the important conspiracy cases and represented his country before international tribunals; Whether it was Iskander Mirza or Ayub Khan, Yahya Khan or Bhutto, no ruler of Pakistan could do without Manzur Qadir.

Last year I spent a day with him in Nathiagali near Murree. He was a very sick man afflicted with phlebitis. But for old times' sake, he drove down to Islamabad to pick me up and drove me back the next evening. I saw for myself the affection and esteem with which he was held by everyone from General Tikka Khan down to the humblest tradesman in the bazaar. It was a continuous shaking of hands and *salam alaikums.*

He bore the pain of his illness with incredible courage and without the slightest attempt to find false props offered by religion. He knew he had a short time to go but had no fear of death. I forget the Urdu couplet he used to quote but it was very much like Wesley's:

If I must die, I will encounter darkness as a bride and hug it in my arms.
When summoned hence to thine eternal sleep, oh, mayest thou smile while all round thee weep.

At our final farewell, the tears were in my eyes, not in his.

An English friend kept me informed of his deteriorating state of health in the London hospital. Apparently she too was not with him when the end came. Tributes to such a man as Manzur Qadir can only be written in tears which leave no stain on paper. He shall be forever honoured and forever mourned. Robert Browning's lines were meant for a man like him:

> We that loved him so, followed him, honoured him,
> Lived in his mild and magnificent age,
> Learned his great language, caught his clear accents,
> Made him our pattern to love and die.

Manzur Qadir died on 12 October 1974.

Some years later, I went to Lahore and stayed as a guest of Asghari (Manzur's wife), son Basharat and his wife Bambi in the house that once was mine. My top priority was to visit my friend's grave. The next morning, accompanied by Basharat and Manzur's old ministers, I went to Lahore's largest Muslim cemetery. We had some difficulty locating the grave we were looking for as there were thousands of them without any clear signs. At last one of the caretakers took us to a cluster of graves where Manzur's parents, Sir Abdul and Lady Qadir, Manzur's uncle M. Sleem, India's number one tennis player for over a dozen years, and Manzur had their final resting place. Basharat had chosen Allama Iqbal's lines for his father's epitaph:

> *Main to jaltee hoon ke muzmir meyree fitrat main soze*
> *Too ferozaan hai keh parvano se ho sanda teyra.*

> (I burn because it is in my nature to do so
> Moths are drawn to you because with warmth you glow.)

KNOWING BHISHAM SAHNI

He was exactly seven days older than I. Though we were in the same class in Government College (Lahore) and lived in the same hostel yet I was hardly aware of his existence. Everyone knew his handsome, elder brother Balraj who later became a film star but Bhisham had no admirers. He was amongst a handful of students who read Hindi. We Urduwalas looked down upon Hindiwalas and called them *kintoo prantoos* (the 'buts' and 'ifs'). After we left college, I hardly ever heard of Bhisham; it was Balraj whose name we liked to drop. The two brothers had two things in common: both were entirely free of communal prejudices and had strong leftist leanings.

Since I could not read Hindi, I did not know how good a writer of Hindi Bhisham had become till he won the Sahitya Akademi Award. I saw bits of his *Tamas* on the screen and realized what I had missed by not knowing its creator as well as I could have. And when he played a role in *Mr & Mrs Iyer* he was as good, if not better than his famous brother in acting. The one and only novel of his that I read and reviewed was *Maya Das Ki Marhi*. I was completely bowled over. When he rang up to thank me, I discovered he lived barely 50 yards away

from me. He was a recluse, almost a hermit. Thereafter I met
him a few times. It was a revelation: the man was totally free
of envy and unlike other writers whose favourite topic is
themselves, Bhisham never talked about himself or his writing.

Bhisham was my classmate; his daughter Kalpana was a
classmate of my daughter Mala and his grandson Martand in
the same class at school as my granddaughter Naina. Kalpana
married the architect Romi Khosla, the youngest son of my
friend G.D. Khosla, Chief Justice of the Punjab and Haryana
High Court, and his wife Shakuntala. So our family
connections went down three generations on either side. I
wish I had known Bhisham Sahni better; he could have made
me a better man.

THE PALAM AIR CRASH: 1973

Three friends gone in one air crash! Satish Loomba I had known since my schooldays and later as a Communist trade unionist at Lahore, Mohan Kumaramangalam at the Inner Temple where we ate our Bar dinners, Gurnam Singh as a lawyer at Lyallpur, leader and philosopher of the Punjabi Suba movement, and Chief Minister of the Punjab. Let me recollect my days with them.

Satish and his brother joined Modern School in Delhi. They looked like identical twins (even in later years I mistook the one for the other). They did not stay very long because their widowed mother was apparently unable to cope with the expenses of boarding two boys at the same time in an expensive elite school.

We found ourselves together again at Government College, Lahore. Satish showed no interest in university politics, but five years later, when I filled my briefless days as Barrister, running the Civil Liberties and Friends of the Soviet Union, Satish was busy organizing workers. It was at his instance that on one occasion, Mr. V.V. Giri as President of the Railwaymen's Union was lodged in my apartment. His disillusionment with the man who was to become Rashtrapati came thirty years before mine.

Satish never minced his words nor hesitated to act when the moment of truth came. For many years as a trade unionist he shied away from the Communist Party. It was only after the war, when Gandhiji, Pandit Nehru, Sardar Patel and other Congress leaders on their release condemned Communists as collaborators, and when everyone knew that they (the Communists) would be inundated under the flood of national anger, that Satish decided to join the Party. Unlike most politicians he did not shut his doors against the setting sun nor hitch his wagon to a rising star. He was an honest man, a hard-working man and as self-effacing as anyone I have known.

Kumaramangalam and I ran into each other at the Bar dinners. Sherry, red wine and port were served, one bottle of each to every group of four boys. Non-drinkers were very popular as their share was taken by those who did. I was then a teetotaller and much in demand by people like Kumaramangalam who was not. He used to wait for me in the foyer where we had to wear our black gowns. 'Hey Sardar! You stay with your black brother,' he used to greet me, and grab me by the shoulder to join his quartet—often consisting of two other non-drinkers. It was not surprising that he was often lit up, loud and full of witticisms. We went back together to King's Cross Station to catch our train. I lived in Welwyn Garden City which was halfway to his destination, Cambridge.

When he was high, which was often, our arguments became shouting matches punctuated with much bawdy abuse. I remember one occasion when I took on two of them. I believe the other was Rajni Patel. They failed to outyell me. Suddenly Mohan threw open the door of the compartment and exhorted Rajni to help him: 'Throw the bastard out of the running train.'

I never met or saw Kumaramangalam after he returned to India, but like everyone else, read about his activities in the papers. When he gave up being a whole-time Party worker to start practice, I was sure he would be a flop. 'Law takes many long years to become lucrative,' I said. After five years at the Bar, I had been unable to make a living. But within a short time, Kumaramangalam began to command an enormous practice. He quit the Party, became Advocate-General and then a Cabinet Minister. But then he had a lot more grey matter than I or most other people have.

I met Gurnam Singh through Manzur Qadir. Both had large practices in Lyallpur and were the closest of friends. When Manzur shifted to Lahore, Gurnam, when he had a case in the High Court, stayed with him. As handsome, cultured and soft-spoken a Sikh as I have ever met. He was, as the cliché goes, elevated to the Bench. On retirement, he elevated himself still higher, using the Punjabi Suba agitation to pedestal himself to triumph. To this day the most lucidly argued and documented case for the Suba is a pamphlet written by Gurnam Singh.

I met him last when as Chief Minister he presided over a session of the P.E.N. Conference at Patiala. The students had organized a demonstration. When the proceedings started, they began to yell slogans and hurl chairs. The police went for them with their batons. Everyone on the stage became excited—everyone save Gurnam. He sat there without an expression on his face, watching the demonstration as if it were on a cinema screen. Later he heard a rendering of Guru Nanak's hymn on the monsoon:

> Sweet sound of water gurgling down the water-spout
> (The peacock's shrill, exultant cry)
> Sister, it's savan, the month of rain!
> Beloved Thine eyes bind me in a spell
> (They pierce through me like daggers)
> They fill my heart with greed and longing;

For one glimpse of Thee I'll give my life
For Thy name art mine, my heart fills with pride,
What can I be proud of if Thou art not with me?
Woman, smash thy bangles on thy bedstead
Break thy arms, break the arms of thy couch;
Thy adornment holds no charms.
Thy Lord is in another's arms.

I do not know why, but Gurnam's eyes filled with tears and he
was unable to make his winding-up speech.

Gurnam was a severe critic of Indira Gandhi and her
government. How he came to be offered the job of High
Commissioner and why he accepted it will remain a murky
mystery.

The death of these three friends reminded me of Thornton
Wilder's novel *The Bridge of San Luis Rey.* He built the story on
the lives of people who, unknown to each other, found
themselves on the bridge at the time it snapped and plunged
them to their doom.

Why did all of them happen to be on the ill-fated Boeing?

PENNY-PINCHING ZINKIN

Maurice Zinkin of the ICS who died last month at 87 was a close friend of Manzur Qadir, who later became Pakistan's Foreign Minister and Chief Justice of Punjab. They were in Cambridge University at the same time.

Every Saturday they would go to the pictures and then dine together. As they boarded a bus to go to the cinema, Maurice would take out his wallet and say, 'Let me pay the bus fare,' and shell out a few pennies for their tickets. It was Manzur's turn to buy the cinema tickets. After the show Maurice would again insist that he pay the bus fare. Then it was Manzur's turn to pay for the dinner. After this had happened a few times, Manzur became wiser and told his friend, 'Maurice, from now on I will pay the bus fares and you pay for the cinema and the dinner.' Thereafter, we referred to Maurice as 'the bus-fare'.

I got to know the Zinkins soon after Maurice got his first posting in India. A year later he had married Taya, more by arrangement made by friends and relatives than love at first sight. He was an English Jew, she French Jewish but with a good command of English.

They came to my wedding reception in 1939 where the

chief attraction was M.A. Jinnah. Taya decided to wear a sari for the first time. She got everything right except she didn't wear a bodice to cover her bra nor a petticoat beneath her sari—which kept slipping off all the time. She pushed her way to the *Qaid-e-Azam* and gushed, 'Mr Jinnah, you are the handsomest man I have ever met.' The Qaid gave her a steely look through his monocle and turned his back towards her. 'He was also the rudest man I ever met,' she told me later.

The Zinkins stayed on in India after Independence. She wrote for *The Manchester Guardian* (later *The Guardian*) and was fiercely resentful of anyone who wrote for the paper. Both wrote books on India. His were highly perceptive on economic matters, hers somewhat frothy on social and political affairs.

I continued to meet the Zinkins whenever I was in London. They belonged to the circle of old India hands who were friendly towards Indians both when they were serving in India and after they had resettled in England. For some reason, both gave up writing and gracefully retired into oblivion.

Taya died a few months after her husband.

I will miss Maurice's scintillating diagnosis of Indian economic ills, and Taya's bitchy comments on Indian politicians.

DAADIMAA: THE PORTRAIT OF A LADY

My grandmother, like everybody's grandmother, was an old woman. She had been old and wrinkled for the twenty years that I had known her. People said that she had once been young and pretty and had even had a husband, but that was hard to believe. My grandfather's portrait hung above the mantelpiece in the drawing room. He wore a big turban and loose-fitting clothes. His long white beard covered the best part of his chest and he looked at least a hundred years old. He did not look the sort of person who would have a wife or children. He looked as if he could only have lots and lots of grandchildren. As for my grandmother being young and pretty, the thought was almost revolting. She often told us of the games she used to play as a child. That seemed quite absurd and undignified on her part and we treated it like the tales of the prophets she used to tell us.

She had always been short and fat and slightly bent. Her face was a crisscross of wrinkles running from everywhere to everywhere. No, we were certain she had always been as we had known her. Old, so terribly old that she could not have grown older, and had stayed at the same age for twenty years.

She could never have been pretty; but she was always beautiful. She hobbled about the house in spotless white with one hand resting on her waist to balance her stoop and the other telling the beads of her rosary. Her silver locks were scattered untidily over her pale, puckered face, and her lips constantly moved in inaudible prayer. Yes, she was beautiful. She was like the winter landscape in the mountains, an expanse of pure white serenity breathing peace and contentment.

My grandmother and I were good friends. My parents left me with her when they went to live in the city and we were constantly together. She used to wake me up in the morning and get me ready for school. She said her morning prayer in a monotonous singsong while she bathed and dressed me in the hope that I would listen and get to know it by heart. I listened because I loved her voice but never bothered to learn it. Then she would fetch my wooden slate which she had already washed and plastered with yellow chalk, a tiny earthen ink pot and a reed pen, tie them all in a bundle and hand it to me. After a breakfast of a thick, stale chapatti with a little butter and sugar spread on it, we went to school. She carried several stale chapattis with her for the village dogs.

My grandmother always went to school with me because the school was attached to the temple. The priest taught us the alphabet and the morning prayer. While the children sat in rows on either side of the verandah singing the alphabet or the prayer in a chorus, my grandmother sat inside reading the scriptures. When we had both finished, we would walk back together. This time the village dogs would meet us at the temple door. They followed us to our home growling and fighting each other for the chapattis we threw to them.

When my parents were comfortably settled in the city, they sent for us. That was a turning point in our friendship. Although we shared the same room, my grandmother no longer

came to school with me. I used to go to an English school in a
motorbus. There were no dogs in the streets and she took to
feeding sparrows in the courtyard of our city house.

As the years rolled by we saw less of each other. For some
time she continued to wake me up and get me ready for
school. When I came back she would ask me what the teacher
had taught me. I would tell her English words and little things
of Western science and learning, the law of gravity,
Archimedes' principle, the world being round, etc. This made
her unhappy. She could not help me with my lessons. She did
not believe in the things they taught at the English school and
was distressed that there was no teaching about God and the
scriptures. One day I announced that we were being given
music lessons. She was very disturbed. To her, music had lewd
associations. It was the monopoly of harlots and beggars and
not meant for gentle folk. She rarely talked to me after that.

When I went up to university, I was given a room of my
own. The common link of friendship was snapped. My
grandmother accepted her seclusion with resignation. She
rarely left her spinning wheel to talk to anyone. From sunrise
to sunset she sat by her wheel spinning and reciting prayers.
Only in the afternoon she relaxed for a while to feed the
sparrows. While she sat in the verandah breaking the bread
into little bits, hundreds of little birds collected around her
creating a veritable bedlam of chirruping. Some came and
perched on her legs, others on her shoulders. Some even sat on
her head. She smiled but never shoo'd them away. It used to
be the happiest half-hour of the day for her.

When I decided to go abroad for further studies, I was sure
my grandmother would be upset. I would be away for five years,
and at her age, one could never tell. But my grandmother could.
She was not even sentimental. She came to see me off at the
railway station but did not talk or show any emotion. Her lips
moved in prayer, her mind was lost in prayer. Her fingers were

busy telling the beads of her rosary. Silently she kissed my forehead, and when I left I cherished the moist imprint as perhaps the last sign of physical contact between us.

But that was not so. After five years I came back home and was met by her at the station. She did not look a day older. She still had no time for words, and while she clasped me in her arms I could hear her reciting her prayer. Even on the first day of my arrival, her happiest moments were with her sparrows whom she fed longer and with frivolous rebukes.

In the evening a change came over her. She did not pray. She collected the women of the neighbourhood, got an old drum and started to sing. For several hours she thumped the sagging skins of the dilapidated drum and sang of the homecoming of warriors. We had to persuade her to stop, to avoid overstraining. That was the first time since I had known her that she did not pray.

The next morning she was taken ill. It was a mild fever and the doctor told us that it would go. But my grandmother thought differently. She told us that her end was near. She said that since only a few hours before the close of the last chapter of her life she had omitted to pray, she was not going to waste any more time talking to us.

We protested. But she ignored our protests. She lay peacefully in bed praying and telling her beads. Even before we could suspect, her lips stopped moving and the rosary fell from her lifeless fingers. A peaceful pallor spread on her face and we knew that she was dead.

It was the summer of 1939.

We lifted her off the bed and, as is customary, laid her on the ground and covered her with a red shroud. After a few hours of mourning we left her alone to make arrangements for her funeral.

In the evening we went to her room with a crude stretcher to take her to be cremated. The sun was setting and had lit her room and verandah with a blaze of golden light. We stopped halfway in the courtyard. All over the verandah and in her room right up to where she lay dead and stiff wrapped in the red shroud, thousands of sparrows sat scattered on the floor. There was no chirping. We felt sorry for the birds and my mother fetched some bread for them. She broke it into little crumbs, the way my grandmother used to, and threw it to them. The sparrows took no notice of the bread. When we carried my grandmother's corpse off, they flew away quietly. Next morning the sweeper swept the breadcrumbs into the dustbin.

CHAJJOO RAM OF RAJ VILLA

Everytime I go to Kasauli, which is at least three times during the summer months, I find one or more of its old residents has passed away. Since the civilian population of Kasauli consists largely of retired old people, this is not very surprising. Also, most of these friendships are summer phenomena: one learns to live without them for the rest of the year. Time and distance lessen the impact of death. Not so in the case of Chajjoo Ram who I had known for over 50 years. Even when I was not in Kasauli, I kept in close touch by telephone and correspondence through his two sons, Thakur Das and Prem, their sons and daughters. In the half century, I learnt to have respect and affection for Chajjoo Ram. His going left a big void in my life.

Chajjoo Ram was born in Goal village of Nalagarh district. He was a Kabir *panthi* (follower of Kabir). I am not sure when he came to Kasauli. He worked with some Sahibs before my father-in-law, Sir Teja Singh Malik, took him on as caretaker of Sperrin Villa, which he had bought from an English spinster and renamed Raj Villa, after his wife. For all practical purposes Raj Villa became Chajjoo Ram's residence for most of the year.

When its owners left for the plains for the winter months, he and his wife Gameero Devi moved into the main house. They looked after it as if it were their own child. One winter, gangs of robbers looted several homes in Kasauli because their caretakers were ordered to stay in servant quarters. They tried to break into Raj Villa as well. But Chajjoo Ram had the presence of mind to shout to his son, *'Mayree bandook leyaana* (get my gun).' He had no gun but the gangsters didn't take any chances and fled.

Once when a forest fire engulfed many houses and came close to Raj Villa, Chajjoo Ram ordered my wife and granddaughter to go to a safer place; he, his wife, sons and grandchildren stood before the advancing fire armed with buckets of water and sticks and beat it back. Again in November 1984, following the assassination of Indira Gandhi, an armed mob from nearby Garkhal went on a rampage, looting and setting fire to Sikh property. A few *goondas* (hoodlums) from Kasauli joined them. Kasauli shopkeepers, all Hindus, barricaded their way. Raj Villa was their prime target. Chajjoo Ram and his sons stood guard at the entrance gate. 'You will have to kill us before you enter this house,' they shouted back. No one dared to take up their challenge.

In the 50 years that Chajjoo Ram lived in Raj Villa, he saw comings and goings of many celebrities: Bhai Vir Singh, Balraj Sahni, Nargis, Sunil and Sanjay Dutt, Salman Haider and his family, Aung San Suu Kyi of Myanmar, and last of all, Protima Bedi. He let them in and looked after them because they came armed with letters from my wife or me. Others, including close relations whom he knew, he refused to allow in: no letter, no admission. As a result not one of the thousands of books, paintings, sculptures and valuable artefacts I have collected has been touched.

We called Chajjoo Ram, Mali Ji. The garden was his primary concern. As long as he was alive, chrysanthemums, sunflowers, gladioli and a dozen other varieties of flowers bloomed around the cottage. He and his dogs fought valiantly against marauding troops of monkeys to preserve the little fruit and vegetables he grew.

As he grew older, he gave up the battle and sat peacefully smoking his hookah in silence. He started to lose weight and apart from putting chairs and table out at dawn and opening windows, had little strength left to do any more. Last April, I noticed a lump come up near his neck. Despite many reminders, he was reluctant to go to a doctor. 'It does not hurt,' he assured me, 'it will go away.'

It didn't. The doctor in Kasauli advised him to go to Shimla and have it examined. His son, Prem, went with him. The reports revealed blood cancer. Every week father and son went to Shimla for a blood transfusion. Last month when I was leaving Kasauli for Delhi, he hobbled down the pathway with a walking stick to see me off. I knew I would not see him any more. I did not. On the morning of Tuesday, 15 September 1998, surrounded by his sisters, sons and their families, he left Raj Villa forever.

SIMBA: FAMILY FAVOURITE

I returned home to Delhi. Once again I was without a job and with very little money in my pocket or in my bank account. All I had on the credit side was a collection of short stories which brought me some good notices but no money, a short and unsatisfactory *Short History of the Sikhs* which was condemned by orthodox Sikhs, and a novel which brought me some money which I had spent. And the manuscript of a second novel which had yet to be accepted by a publisher.

Amongst those who greeted me at home was a one-month old Alsatian pup presented by a friend of my father's to my daughter, Mala. To start with, he resented me as an intruder in his tight little human family consisting of my wife and our two children. He slept in the same upstairs bedroom in my father's house and used the roof of the porch as his lavatory. Till then he had no name. I decided to name him Simba after the marmalade cat we had abandoned in Paris. As with most Alsatians, Simba was a one-person dog. He belonged to my daughter, my wife fed him, took him to the vet for his shots and for any ailment he had, but he adopted me as his master. He was as human a dog as I have ever known and shared our joys as he did our sorrows. By the time we moved into our own ground-floor apartment in Sujan Singh Park, he had got over his frisky 'puppiness' and grown into a powerful full-sized German Shepherd. He still shared our bedroom, where he had his own cot. And for his sake more than ours we had an air-conditioner put in the room. Often at night he would sniff into my ears and ask me to make room for him. I did. He would heave himself on to the bed with a deep sigh of gratitude, and take over more than half of my bed for the rest of the night.

We would talk to him. If we pretended to cry, he would sniff soothingly in our ears and join us wailing: *booo, ooo ooo.* If he was naughty, we'd order him to the corner. He stayed there with his head down in penitence till we said, 'Okay, now you can come back.'

Simba developed a special relationship with Mala's ayah, the seventy-five-year-old Mayee. 'Vey Shambia!' she would greet him as she opened the door to let Simba out in the garden. She waited for him to do his business in the garden before going to the neighbouring gurdwara to say her prayers. He knew he was not allowed inside the gurdwara and sat outside guarding her slippers. Just as the morning prayer was about to end, he would take one of her slippers in his mouth, trot home and hide it under a bed. Mayee would follow him pleading, 'Vey Shambia! Where have you hidden my slipper?' He followed her from room to room wagging his tail till she found the missing slipper.

Simba was always impatient for his evening walk. He would put his head in my lap and look appealingly at me: 'Isn't it time?' his eyes asked. 'Not yet,' I would reply. Then he would bring his leash and put it at my feet. 'Now?' I would tell him not to be so impatient. Next he brought my walking stick and dropped it on the book I was reading. 'Surely now!' There was no escape. He whined and trembled with excitement as we left. As he jumped on to the rear seat of the car his whining became louder. He liked to put his head out of the window and bark challenges to every dog, cow or bull we passed on the road. He had to be let off at the entrance of the Lodhi Gardens. He raced the car, stopping briefly to defecate, and resumed the race to the parking lot. At that time there used to be some hares in the park. He would sniff them out of the hedges and then go in hot pursuit, yelping as he tried to catch up with them. They were too fast and dodgy for him. But he became quite adept at hunting squirrels. He learnt that they ran to the nearest tree and went round its bole to evade pursuit. He would steal up to the tree and then go for them. In the open ground they had no escape. However much I reprimanded him and even beat him, he could not resist killing harmless squirrels.

On Saturday evenings he could sense from the picnic basket being packed that the next day would be devoted largely to him. Long before dawn he would start whimpering with excitement and wake everyone up. It was difficult to control him in the car. When we got to the open countryside near Suraj Kund, or Tilpat, we had to let him out to prevent him from jumping out of the car. He would chase herds of cows and scatter them over the fields. Once he nearly got his face bashed in by the rear kick of a cow. And once he almost killed a goat.

Three to four hours in the open countryside chasing hares, deer or peafowl made him happily tired. It was a drowsy, sleepy Simba we brought back from our Sunday morning picnics. He was not so impatient now for his evening walk.

He was, again, restless for his after-dinner stroll round Khan Market, where we went to get *paan*. He would stop by the ice-cream man and plead with us to buy him one. He was passionately fond of ice-cream. He was also very possessive. Once somebody had two lovely pups for sale under a tree in the market. He resented our paying attention to them. Whenever we stopped by the tree he would savagely bite its bole. Everyone in and around Sujan Singh Park knew Simba. We came to be known by the children of the locality as Simba's parents.

Simba was also feared. Once when going out with my wife and daughter in the Lodhi Gardens, a cyclist slapped my daughter on her back and sped on. My wife screamed, 'Simba get him!' Simba chased the man, knocked him off his bicycle and stood over him baring his fangs. The poor fellow folded the palms of his hands and pleaded forgiveness. Another time, as I was stepping out of my flat after dinner, I heard a girl shout for help. Two young lads were trying to molest her. 1 ran towards her with Simba following on my heels. The boys tried to run away. I ordered Simba to get them. He ran and brought one fellow down on the ground. He was a big fellow and much stronger than I. But with Simba at my side, I had no hesitation in slapping the man many times across his face and roundly abusing him, calling him a *goonda* and a *badmaash*. He asked to be forgiven and swore he would never make passes at women again.

We always took Simba with us to Mashobra or Kasauli. He was happiest in the mountains. I often put him on the leash to make him pull us up steep inclines. He liked Kasauli more than Shimla because of its herds of rhesus monkeys and langoors. He waged unceasing warfare against them, and against hill crows which flocked round when he was having his afternoon meal.

Most dogs have a sixth sense. Our Simba had seventh and eighth senses as well. I will mention only one episode to prove it. My wife and I had to go abroad for a couple of months. Our children were in boarding schools. We decided to give our servants leave and lock up our flat. Simba was to be housed with Prem Kirpal: the two were on very friendly terms, as Prem was always with us on our Sunday outings and a regular visitor to our home. He happily agreed to take Simba. Being a senior government official, he had a bungalow on Canning Lane with a large garden. Simba had been there many times and sensed that we meant to leave him there. He did not seem to mind very much.

My wife returned to Delhi a few days before me. She went to Canning Lane to fetch Simba. He greeted her joyfully but refused to get into her car. Prem was very pleased over his success in winning Simba's affections. My wife reluctantly gave in. 'If he is happy with you, he can stay here,' she said. Apparently they mentioned the date I was due to return, and Simba heard them. The evening before I returned to Delhi, Simba walked all the way from Canning Lane to Sujan Singh Park and scratched at the door with his paws to announce his arrival. He knew I was coming next morning. Prem was more dejected at Simba leaving him than he would have been had I stolen his mistress.

Simba aged gracefully. The hair about his mouth turned white. He developed cataract. Sometimes he got feverish: there were times when my wife spent whole nights with his head on her lap, stroking his head. He was then well over thirteen years old. When I got a three-month teaching assignment at Swarthmore College, we had to leave him in the care of his real mistress, my daughter Mala. She had to take him to the vet almost every day. He didn't get any better. His legs began to give in. She sent us a cable 'Return immediately, Simba seriously ill.' The next day, we received another cable from Mala: 'Simba passed away peacefully.'

Apparently, the vet advised Mala that Simba was in pain, his legs were paralyzed and he couldn't last much longer. With her permission, on 20 March 1969, he gave him a lethal dose of something which put him to sleep.

If I had to talk of my close friendships, Simba would be amongst the top in my list. We never kept another dog. One can't replace friends.

EPITAPH: KHUSHWANT SINGH

Here lies one who spared neither man nor God
Waste not your tears on him, he was a sod
Writing nasty things he regarded as great fun
Thank the Lord he is dead, this son of a gun.

INDEX